C000261125

BRIGHTON

Ellie Seymour

PHOTOGRAPHS

Emma Croman, Lyndsey Haskell, Lucy Sharpe and Dan Seymour

JONGLEZ PUBLISHING

travel guides

Ellie Seymour is a journalist who has lived in Brighton for 15 years. She writes about the city's curiosities and hidden places on her blog Ellie & Co., Inc, which she started as a way to rediscover Brighton away from the tourist crowds. She cannot walk past an intriguing alleyway or courtyard without seeing what's on the other side – and is always looking for the next adventure or hidden place to write about.

We have taken great pleasure in drawing up *Secret Brighton* and hope that through its guidance you will, like us, continue to discover unusual, hidden or little-known aspects of the city. Some entries are accompanied by historical asides or anecdotes as an aid to understanding the city in all its complexity.

Secret Brighton also draws attention to the multitude of details found in places that we may pass every day without noticing. We invite you to look more closely at the urban landscape and to see your own city with the curiosity and attention that we often display while travelling elsewhere …

Comments on this guidebook and its contents, as well as information on places we may not have mentioned, are more than welcome and will enrich future editions.

Don't hesitate to contact us:
E-mail: info@jonglezpublishing.com
Jonglez Publishing
25 rue du Maréchal Foch
78000 Versailles, France

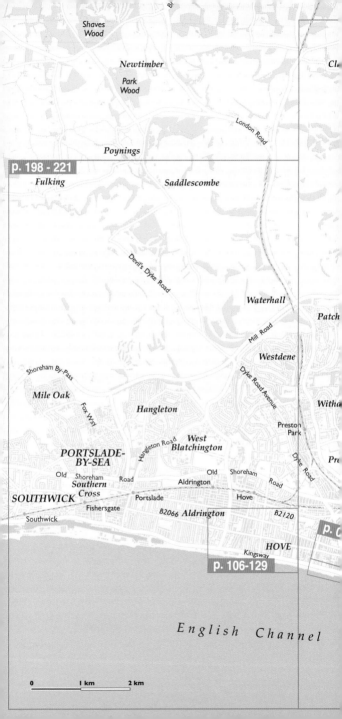

Shaves
Wood

Newtimber

Park
Wood

Cl

London Road

Poynings

p. 198 - 221

Fulking

Saddlescombe

Devil's Dyke Road

Waterhall

Patch

Mill Road

Westdene

Dyke Road Avenue

Shoreham By-Pass

Mile Oak

Fox Way

Hangleton

Preston
Park

Witha

Dyke Road

Pre

PORTSLADE-
BY-SEA

Hangleton Road

West
Blatchington

Old   Shoreham   Road

Old   Shoreham   Road

Southern
Cross

Aldrington

Hove

p. (

SOUTHWICK

Portslade

B2066 Aldrington

B2120

Southwick

Fishersgate

HOVE

Kingsway

p. 106-129

English   Channel

0   1 km   2 km

Beacon Road

B2116

Plumpton

Warningore Wood

Westmeston

Ditchling Road

Highpark Wood

Millbank Wood

Stanmer

Great Wood

Falmer

Coldean

Falmer

ad

North Moulsecoomb

B2123

HTON HOVE

p. 130-161

oulsecoomb

Bevendean

Bear Road

Warren Road

Woodingdean

m Grove

Freshfield Road

Whitehawk

Wilson Avenue

Kemptown

Ovingdean

Falmer Road

Greenways

p. 021-045

Roedean

Rottingdean

Saltdean

CONTENTS

Brighton Seafront

ANGEL OF PEACE STATUE	14
BRIGHTON AND HOVE PÉTANQUE CLUB	15
THE SKY LOUNGE	16
ELECTRIC LIGHTING PLAQUE	18
EUGENIUS BIRCH PLAQUE	20
THE CLARENCE SUITE	22
"MURMURATION" AERIAL SHOW	24
BRIGHTON'S VICTORIAN SEWERS	26
BRIGHTON MUSIC TUNNEL	28
BRIGHTON PALACE PIER HERITAGE TRAIL	30
ROYAL SUSPENSION CHAIN PIER REMAINS	32
ATHINA-B ANCHOR	34
FLINT GROTTO	36
MADEIRA LIFT	38
MAGNUS VOLK'S FORMER OFFICE AND WORKSHOP	40
MADEIRA DRIVE GREEN WALL	42
BLACKROCK SUBWAY STUDIOS	44

Central Brighton

WESTERN PAVILION	48
CONSTABLE'S FORMER HOME	50
ANNA'S MUSEUM	52
ST NICHOLAS REST GARDEN BURIAL VAULTS	54
FRENCH PROTESTANT CHURCH	56
"TWINS" SOUND-AND-LIGHT SCULPTURE	58
"WRITE AROUND AIR STREET" ART STORY TRAIL	60
TIME BALL	62
FABRICA GALLERY	64
BRIGHTON HIPPODROME	66
MIDDLE STREET SYNAGOGUE	68
OLD SHIP ASSEMBLY ROOMS	70

THEATRE ROYAL BACKSTAGE TOURS 72

MAX MILLER STATUE 74

CERES SCULPTURE 76

BRIGHTON DOME BACKSTAGE TOURS 78

HENRY SOLOMON PLAQUE 80

OLD POLICE CELLS MUSEUM 82

QUADROPHENIA ALLEY 84

INDIA GATE 86

THE DRAWING CIRCUS 88

ROYAL PAVILION BASEMENT AND TUNNELS 90

PRINNY'S PIANO 92

ART DECO BUS SHELTER 94

FORMER HOME OF MARIA FITZHERBERT 96

DR RUSSELL PLAQUE 98

SCHOOL OF SCIENCE AND ART TERRACOTTA FRIEZES 100

UNIVERSITY OF BRIGHTON DESIGN ARCHIVES 102

WASTE HOUSE 104

Central Hove

JAIPUR GATE 108

EVEREST'S GRAVE 110

ORNATE INTERIOR OF THE SACRED HEART CHURCH 112

THE HOVE CLUB 114

THE JUGGLER STATUE 115

33 PALMEIRA MANSIONS 116

BODHISATTVA KADAMPA MEDITATION CENTRE 118

WINSTON CHURCHILL PLAQUE 120

THE REGENCY TOWN HOUSE 122

HEADLESS STATUE 124

WATERLOO STREET ARCH AND GARDEN 126

ST ANDREW'S CHURCH 128

CONTENTS

Kemptown to Whitehawk

LITTLE FRIDGE LIBRARY	132
AIDS MEMORIAL SCULPTURE	134
TOMB TRAIL	136
FEIBUSCH NATIVITY MURAL	138
THE PEPPERPOT	140
ATTREE VILLA TEMPLE	142
ST LUKE'S VICTORIAN SWIMMING BATHS	144
ROYAL SPA REMAINS	146
KEMP TOWN RAILWAY TUNNEL	148
FISHERMEN'S GALLERY	150
PEEL FAMILY CRYPT	152
SASSOON MAUSOLEUM	154
WHITEHAWK HILL	156
RACEHILL COMMUNITY ORCHARD	158
SECRET GARDEN KEMP TOWN	160

North Laine to Round Hill

THE GHOST OF JENNY LIND SCULPTURE	164
RICHARDSON'S YARD	166
BRIGHTON GREENWAY	168
ANTIQUE SAFE AT THE DUKE'S	170
CAMDEN TERRACE	172
BRIGHTON TOY AND MODEL MUSEUM	174
SUSSEX MASONIC CENTRE	176
LOAVES AND FISHES SCULPTURE	178
JEW STREET	180
THE OLD VICARAGE	182
FORMER ISETTA FACTORY SITE	184
SILVER ALTAR	186
THE GARDEN HOUSE	188
MAX MILLER ROOM	190

IRELAND'S GARDENS GATEWAY 192
ROUND HILL CATS' CREEP 193
SHOE TREE 194
BENJAMIN JAMES SMITH HOUSE 196

Hove Park to Portslade

MILE OAK FARM 200
FOREDOWN TOWER 202
PORTSLADE MANOR RUINS 204
ST MARYE'S CONVENT BURIAL GROUND 206
SECRET GARDEN 208
DINO THE ELEPHANT SCULPTURE 210
HOVE LAGOON MODEL YACHT CLUB 212
THE CIRCUS PROJECT 214
WEST BLATCHINGTON WINDMILL 216
HOVE PARK MINIATURE RAILWAY 218
THE GOLDSTONE 220

Patcham to Rottingdean

CHATTRI MEMORIAL 224
PATCHAM PEACE GARDEN 226
DOROTHY STRINGER SCHOOL BUTTERFLY HAVEN 228
PRESTON MANOR 230
BONE GUILLOTINE 232
ROYAL CREST 234
ST PETER'S CHURCH 236
PRESTON WELL HOUSE 238
PRESTON MANOR PET CEMETERY 240
PRESTON MANOR WALLED GARDEN 242
THE "PRESTON TWINS" 244

CONTENTS

BOOTH MUSEUM OF NATURAL HISTORY   *246*

BACKSTAGE AT THE BOOTH MUSEUM OF NATURAL HISTORY   *248*

THE CASCADE   *250*

STEVE OVETT'S FOOT   *252*

K6 PHONE BOXES   *254*

RICHARD'S GARAGE   *256*

TAKE SHELTER! MUSEUM   *258*

REGENCY DRAGONFLIES   *260*

FLORENCE PLACE JEWISH BURIAL GROUND   *262*

HOLLINGBURY HILLFORT   *264*

WILD PARK   *266*

EARTHSHIP BRIGHTON   *268*

URBAN FORAGING   *270*

WOODINGDEAN WELL   *272*

GLOBALLS JURASSIC MINIATURE GOLF   *274*

BRIGHTON WALK OF FAME   *276*

DADDY LONG LEGS REMAINS   *278*

THE HEAD OF DAVID JACOBS   *280*

WISHING STONE   *282*

ST MARGARET'S CHURCH   *283*

THE KIPLING ROOM   *284*

BALSDEAN ABANDONED VILLAGE   *286*

HARVEY'S CROSS   *288*

UNUSUAL BARS, CAFÉS AND RESTAURANTS   *290*

ALPHABETICAL INDEX   *298*

Brighton Seafront

1. ANGEL OF PEACE STATUE — 14
2. BRIGHTON AND HOVE PÉTANQUE CLUB — 15
3. THE SKY LOUNGE — 16
4. ELECTRIC LIGHTING PLAQUE — 18
5. EUGENIUS BIRCH PLAQUE — 20
6. THE CLARENCE SUITE — 22
7. "MURMURATION" AERIAL SHOW — 24
8. BRIGHTON'S VICTORIAN SEWERS — 26
9. BRIGHTON MUSIC TUNNEL — 28

⑩	BRIGHTON PALACE PIER HERITAGE TRAIL	30
⑪	ROYAL SUSPENSION CHAIN PIER REMAINS	32
⑫	ATHINA-B ANCHOR	34
⑬	FLINT GROTTO	36
⑭	MADEIRA LIFT	38
⑮	MAGNUS VOLK'S FORMER OFFICE AND WORKSHOP	40
⑯	MADEIRA DRIVE GREEN WALL	42
⑰	BLACKROCK SUBWAY STUDIOS	44

ANGEL OF PEACE STATUE

An elegant Victorian boundary marker

Kingsway, Hove BN3 2WN

Set between Brunswick Lawns and the Esplanade, opposite the grand homes of Brunswick Terrace, stands the Angel of Peace – or the Peace Statue, as locals often refer to it. This Grade II-listed monument sits on the boundary between Brighton and Hove.

It was commissioned primarily as a memorial to King Edward VII, the eldest son of Queen Victoria, known as "The Peacemaker" for his efforts to maintain world peace. He's also thought to have convalesced several times in Brighton, adding to its fashionable reputation.

The 9-metre-high bronze statue depicts a winged female angel of peace facing north. It stands on a globe supported by dolphin-like figures set on a tall stone pedestal. The angel holds an orb in her left hand and an olive branch in her right. A bronze plaque decorates each side of the pedestal – one each depicting the Hove and Brighton coats of arms, one commemorating Edward VII's reign and another acknowledging the date the statue was erected. This large-scale artwork is a good example of the Victorian tradition of publicly funded art and is one of several pieces around the Hove seafront area. It was designed by Royal College of Art and Royal Academy trained artist, Newbury Abbot Trent, who specialised in war memorials and whose work includes similar angel pieces. He was chosen from the 18 artists and companies who competed for the commission.

The Duke of Norfolk unveiled the monument in October 1912, on the same day that a new home for the Queen's Nurses was opened in Wellington Road, in the Hanover area of Brighton – also in memory of the late King Edward VII. A wooden model of Abbot Trent's statue stood in its place until the real thing was put up.

NEARBY

Brighton and Hove Pétanque Club ②

www.bhpetanque.org

Across from the statue is an open space known as the Peace Statue Terrain. This is a large pétanque ground where the Brighton and Hove Pétanque Club meet every Saturday and Sunday afternoon year-round from 1pm and often on Wednesday evenings in summer.

Boundary stone

At the junction of Boundary Passage and Montpelier Place in Hove is another boundary marker, albeit far less ornate. Dating back to the 19th century, this rectangular marker is made of granite and stands 50 cm high. It has a faceted top, a boundary line cut into the sides and across the top, and the inscription "BP" for Boundary Passage on its front face.

THE SKY LOUNGE

Reminiscent of an old ocean liner

Embassy Court, King's Road, Brighton BN1
Open during the Brighton Festival in May, Heritage Open Days weekends in
September and for private tours
www.embassycourt.org.uk/contact-us/

Known as the "Sky Lounge", the incredible balcony on the 11th floor of the Grade II-listed Embassy Court arguably offers one of the most enviable views over Brighton and Hove seafront.

Today, it's mainly a communal space for residents and also the final destination on a tour of this fascinating iconic seafront landmark, which lay rotting after years of neglect until it was restored in 2005.

Embassy Court was designed in 1935 by expat Canadian architect Wells Coates as an architectural experiment in modernism and was aimed at an upmarket clientele. In the brief pre-war era when it operated, it was one of the most prestigious apartment buildings in the UK. Its occupants are said to have included Laurence Olivier, Rex Harrison and Graham Greene, who shot to fame with his novel about the area, Brighton Rock.

The 72 flats were initially only available to rent. Prices ranged from £155 a year for a one-bedroom flat with a reception room, bathroom, toilet and small kitchen, up to £500 a year for a three-bedroom flat with two receptions, two bathrooms, two toilets and a kitchen – a year's rent would have bought a whole house in Brighton at the time.

The tour takes you all around the building, starting in the lobby, which has interesting features such as an old telephone booth and the entrance to the former on-site bank. It includes a trip in a tiny old passenger lift – in 1936, the building had a staff of 35, including one full-time senior caretaker, two other caretakers, as well as cooks and cleaners, so occupants would not have carried their own shopping or luggage upstairs!

The tour also takes in an apartment for a look at some classic Wells Coates detailing, including curved doors and door handles. Note the tiny kitchens, as residents would mainly have eaten out, or in the former ground-floor restaurant.

The Sky Lounge is accessed through the "tank room", which once housed a giant boiler for the centralised heating system. It is now a communal space for residents and has a small museum of artefacts relating to the building's heritage, including a 1930s TV unearthed recently in one of the apartments.

A blue plaque outside Embassy Court, and a small exhibition in the lobby, pay tribute to Brighton-born Edward Zeff. This Jewish undercover Allied spy survived torture at the hands of the Nazis and moved into Embassy Court after the war.

ELECTRIC LIGHTING PLAQUE

A faded reminder of a powerful day in Brighton's history

King's Road, close to the West Pier

Even the most trained spotter of unusual city sights might fail to notice this faded, nondescript plaque hidden on the side of an old cast-iron lamppost near the West Pier (see p. 20). It commemorates the introduction of electric lighting to Brighton seafront on 16 September 1893, with the installation of 41 lampposts, "in a ceremony performed by a Miss Ewart, Mayoress of Brighton".

Until then, gas had been used to illuminate the towns of Brighton and Hove, replacing oil lamps in around 1818. Electricity was introduced in 1881, first to the Grand Hotel and then to Brighton station, although the supply was unrefined, unreliable and expensive.

In 1891, however, the Brighton Corporation – now Brighton & Hove City Council – obtained the go-ahead to set up an electricity-generating station in North Road. This changed the city's lighting landscape for good, providing Brighton and Hove with a reliable and permanent electricity source. It also meant that seafront lighting could be installed.

This new row of 41 lampposts was considered the town's first major lighting scheme ... and possibly the most expensive. It was claimed that the "gorgeous electric lamps" gave 10 times more light than gas.

To ensure that the ceremony went smoothly, "the Corporation had taken the precaution of trying out the lamps in the early hours", according to local historian Judy Middleton's blog, Hove in the Past. "The evening of the grand switch-on was one of drizzling rain and so only a few spectators gathered at the foot of Regency Square to see the ceremony. When switched on, 'one lamp refused to act for 10 minutes, but finally settled down to a career of steady progress'."

Today, it's thought there are around 1,800 cast-iron lampposts left in the city, reflecting its lighting heritage. Painted cream and Cambridge blue, although they might look identical at first glance, they're all very different in style and bear different decorations, such as coats of arms, flowers, or the maker's name. Only around 140 are listed.

He may be famous for his Electric Railway and outlandish inventions, especially the ill-fated Daddy Long Legs (see p. 278), but what's less well known is that Magnus Volk made another contribution to the city: he introduced electric lighting to the Banqueting Room in the Royal Pavilion on 3 April 1883.

EUGENIUS BIRCH PLAQUE

Remembering the engineer of the West Pier

King's Road, Brighton BN1 2FL
www.westpier.co.uk

f there's one structure that most represents Brighton's Victorian seaside heyday, it could be the West Pier. Although only a ghostly charred skeleton is left, these remains have become the most distinctive feature of Brighton's seafront and the city's most photographed landmark.

However, most people entranced by its otherworldly beauty might not notice the new and little-known plaque commemorating its famous designer, Eugenius Birch – it's embedded in the ground in the middle of a seafront sculpture constructed out of old West Pier pillars.

A 19th-century seaside architect and civil engineer, Birch and his brother built railways, bridges and viaducts across England. He also travelled to India to build railways for the East Indian Railway Company – a trip some say influenced the oriental design of his masterpiece, Brighton's West Pier.

The West Pier opened in 1866 as a simple promenade pier with an open deck and six small oriental-style ornamental houses. By the early 20th century, with the addition of a theatre and concert hall, it had become a thriving centre of seaside entertainment. The year 1919 recorded the highest-ever figure of 2,074,000 paying visitors.

By the late 1920s, the fully developed West Pier was enjoying its glamorous heyday. In 1975, however, it was closed for safety reasons. In March 2003, before dreams of a newly renovated West Pier could be realised, its main pavilion was destroyed by fire. Another fire, two months later, destroyed the concert hall.

The original tollbooths from the West Pier have been rebuilt and are used as kiosks that flank the British Airways i360 observation tower – this opened in summer 2016, close to the West Pier remains. There are plans for an original 1866 octagonal kiosk salvaged in the late 1990s to be restored and turned into a West Pier heritage centre, as part of the i360 experience; this would allow visitors to experience at first hand a key part of the original pier.

You'll find a bench from the original West Pier in the Secret Garden in Kemp Town (see p. 160).

THE CLARENCE SUITE

A historic ballroom in a former chapel

Hilton Brighton Metropole, Kings Road, Brighton BN1 2FU
www.hilton.com/brightonmet
Available for private hire, viewing strictly by appointment
To book a visit, call 01273 720710 or email: enquiries.brightonmet@hilton.com

Hidden deep within the Metropole Hotel's complex of conference halls is a secret historic entertainment space set inside a beautiful old chapel dating back to 1820.

The hotel was designed and built in 1890 by the architect of London's Natural History Museum, Alfred Waterhouse, on a site next door to the chapel. He incorporated it into his design, surrounding it with a stunning Italian-style garden. With its barrel-vaulted ceiling and three chandeliers, it became a magnificent function room for private events called the Clarence Room, named after the nearby Clarence Square.

It had its own entrance on Canon Place and in its heyday was the setting for Cinderella-style balls, dances, banquets and wedding celebrations. Through a door leading off the Clarence Room was another impressive space known as a "crush room", where guests would go to rest

and enjoy light refreshments in between dances. This was demolished and rebuilt in the 1960s and today is known as the Lancaster Suite.

When the Metropole opened, luxury trains were chartered from London Victoria for the 1,500 extra visitors. A special red "carpet" made of sand was spread along Kings Road for VIP guests. The opening day was the beginning of a golden era for Brighton hotels that would last until the late 1930s. With its 700 rooms and a banqueting room big enough to hold 500 diners, the Metropole was Brighton's largest and most prestigious hotel, as well as the nation's largest hotel outside London.

As the type of visitors to Brighton changed, the hotel's owner at the time, Mr Harold Poster, saw its future as a conference venue. After a redevelopment in the 1960s, the Clarence Suite became famous as the country's first licensed continental-style casino. It counts Ian Fleming, author of the James Bond story, *Casino Royale*, as one of its most famous early guests. In its first two weeks, £500,000 was won and lost at the gaming tables. By 1967, the casino was still taking what was the staggering sum of £70,000 a night. It moved to an address on nearby Preston Street in 1985, but the Clarence Suite has remained a function room, as it has been for the past 13 decades.

"MURMURATION" AERIAL SHOW

A swooping spectacle of starlings

Can be viewed along the seafront, usually between the piers

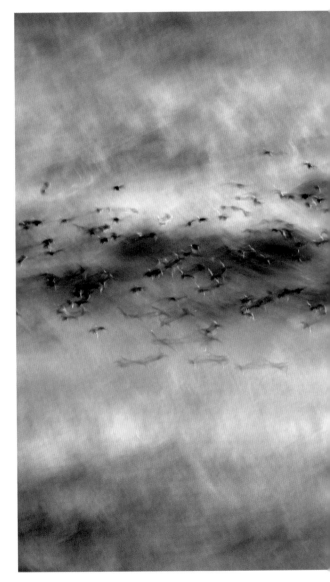

Brighton is the setting for one of the most beautiful natural sights in the world. On most winter days, around 20 minutes before sunrise, and again 20 minutes before sunset, thousands and thousands of starlings perform a spellbinding aerial show known as "murmuration".

It can usually be viewed anywhere along the seafront between the two piers or on Brighton Palace Pier itself. On a calm evening, you can even hear the flutter of wings as the swooping mass of birds whirls in the sky above, as they gather over their roosting site, performing stunts before they bed down for the night.

According to the Royal Society for the Protection of Birds (RSPB), starlings do this for many different reasons. For example, grouping together offers safety in numbers – predators such as peregrine falcons find it hard to target one bird in the middle of a hypnotising flock of thousands. The birds also gather to keep warm at night and to exchange information, such as on good feeding areas.

Autumn roosts usually begin to form in November, although this varies from site to site and some can start as early as September. More and more birds will flock together as the weeks go by. The number of starlings in a roost can sometimes swell to around 100,000.

At night, the starlings roost in places sheltered from harsh weather and predators, such as woodlands, but reed beds, cliffs, buildings and industrial structures are also used. During the day, however, they form daytime roosts at exposed places such as treetops, where they have good all-round visibility.

Despite the incredible size of the flocks, the RSPB reports that starling numbers are just a fraction of what they used to be, the population having fallen by over 80 per cent in recent years. This means that starlings are now on the critical list of UK birds most at risk.

In 2015, Brighton-based wildlife photographer Andrew Forsyth was a finalist in the Wildlife Photographer of the Year competition with one of his photos of starling murmurations in Brighton. Murmurations are a popular subject for photographers and Forsyth spent months at the end of Brighton Palace Pier trying to capture them in a new and unusual way. This included venturing out in gale force winds (including 113 km/h gusts) and taking hundreds of photos in treacherous conditions. Visit www.thewildlifephotographer.com to discover more about Forsyth's work.

BRIGHTON'S VICTORIAN SEWERS

An exceptional feat of underground engineering

King's Arches, 256 King's Road, Brighton BN2 1TD
Tel: 01903 272124
www.southernwater.co.uk/brighton-sewer-tours
Open: May–Sept for tours

The city's Victorian sewer system was so well designed that it remains in use today. Arch number 260 underneath the Brighton Palace Pier is the meeting place for one of the city's most obscure, yet surprisingly popular tours: it takes visitors through a 366-metre section of the 48-km system, starting at the Brighton Palace Pier and emerging through a manhole in the middle of Old Steine Gardens.

The visit begins with a historical introduction to the sewers and Victorian Brighton. Although today this is a Mecca of arty boutiques, it was once a slum-like village full of fishermen's cottages. The sewage ran into the streets through storm drains into the sea, sometimes seeping through the cottages' chalky foundations into the basement walls, and gradually filling up the houses.

When London's bourgeoisie started visiting the coast, demanding luxury, something had to be done about the sewage. All through the mid-1800s, most of it drained into cesspools at the back of the houses. Finally, the council decided enough was enough and set about creating a new system.

Sir John Hawkshaw's incredible brick-lined sewers are an ingenious feat of Victorian engineering. With no hydraulic diggers or power tools, the sewer system was built solely by hand. The bricklayers of the 1870s were paid between 10 and 15 shillings (50p to 75p) per 12 ft (3.7 metres) length of the sewer tunnel, depending how thick the brickwork was. The best men could earn £4 and 10 shillings a week, while general labourers earned half the bricklayers' pay.

Until the 1990s, the system transported the sewage away from Brighton beach east to a little place called Portobello on Telscombe Cliffs, where it flowed into the sea. Today, it flows to the new £300 million sewage treatment works in Peacehaven.

Look closely at the brickwork in the sewer tunnels and you'll see shells encrusted in the mortar – a clue that Victorian bricklayers took hundreds of tonnes of sand from the beach to make the "pug" to cement the millions of bricks.

BRIGHTON MUSIC TUNNEL

An underground art gallery

Brighton Sea Life Centre, Marine Parade, Brighton BN2 1TB

A previously dull and featureless underground pedestrian walkway that stretches from the Sea Life Centre to the beach-side of Marine Parade near the King's Road Arches, the Brighton Music Tunnel now boasts a stunning 24-metre mural on its inside walls.

The tunnel was the brainchild of Brighton record producer and songwriter David Courtney, founder of the Walk of Fame at Brighton Marina and the Music Walk of Fame on the Brighton Palace Pier (see p. 276). He wanted to pay homage to a once thriving 1960s Brighton music venue called The Florida Rooms, Britain's first R&B club. Featured in the film *Quadrophenia*, the club once formed part of the site now occupied by the Sea Life Centre.

Created by local students, the mural is a riot of colour depicting various stars of the Brighton music scene, past and present. These include Brighton's own DJ and producer Norman Cook (aka Fat Boy Slim), Nick Cave and Roger Daltrey, who played at the club's regular Wednesday-night sessions when The Who were an up-and-coming band. According to the website *Brighton Beat*, Rod Stewart, Chris Barber and Screaming Lord Sutch also played here.

One-time Brighton resident Sir Paul McCartney and local band The Levellers also feature in the mural. You'll find them alongside Swedish pop band Abba, who won their Eurovision Song Contest crown here in 1974 with an unforgettable performance of *Waterloo* at the Brighton Dome, an event that has recently been honoured with a blue plaque outside the venue's main entrance on Church Street.

Roger Daltrey opened the artwork with a live performance on 25 May 2010.

You can read students' accounts of their work creating the mural at www.tunnelvisionbrighton.blogspot.co.uk

The Brighton Music Tunnel was featured in a 2010 documentary on BBC 1 called *Brighton, the First Resort* (part of the *History of the World* series). Hosted by Suggs from the band Madness, the programme looks at Brighton's musical and cultural heritage and includes an interview with David Courtney about his plans to transform the tunnel into an underground art gallery.

BRIGHTON PALACE PIER HERITAGE TRAIL

The history of Brighton Palace Pier

Brighton Palace Pier, Madeira Drive, Brighton BN2 1TW
Open daily, 10am–10pm
Admission free

f you can bear to fight through the swathes of visitors and giant tour groups, and ignore the endless tackiness of Brighton's most famous tourist attraction, the Brighton Palace Pier Heritage Trail offers an alternative and little-known way to appreciate it.

Almost all locals and visitors traipse around the pier's sweet shops, amusement arcades and rides, stopping for fish and chips in the Palm Court and drinks in Horatio's Bar. Lured by candyfloss and the carousel, they are unaware of the delights of the heritage trail.

But scattered around the pier and hidden in plain sight, mostly on the beautiful wrought-iron railings, the heritage trail placards offer some escape from the rampart commercialism. They tell the story of Brighton Palace Pier from its inception to the present day.

It's the little snippets of information about the pier's heyday that are arguably the most intriguing – they allow us to time-travel away from the stench of fried donuts and the ear-piercing fairground tunes, to a time when a wander along the Brighton Marine Palace & Pier was a genteel affair. During this era, visitors could catch a show in its beautiful winter garden, the setting for regular live music performances; today, home to the Palace of Fun amusement arcade.

We also learn about the "pier masters" who, up until the 1970s, were in charge of running the pier – in the early years, they were chosen for their nautical skills. "The longest-serving pier master was a Captain Weeks, who served from 1928 to 1953, having spent 25 years at sea before he joined. He wore a gold braided uniform with three rings on the sleeve and a row of war ribbons on his chest, while the men under his command were known as the crew," reveals one plaque.

Perhaps the most significant inclusion is at plaque nine, towards the middle of the pier on the right – an old Signal Cannon once located on the Royal Suspension Chain Pier (see p. 32). It now sits alongside two of its original kiosks that were located on the shore, and are today used as toilets.

A number of original square kiosks remain along the length of the pier. Most are marked with the initials "BMPP", which refer to its original name, Brighton Marine Palace & Pier.

ROYAL SUSPENSION CHAIN PIER REMAINS

Submerged remnants of Brighton's first pier

Madeira Drive, Brighton BN2

f you look closely at the shoreline in front of the Sea Life Centre at extremely low tide, you might see some wooden stumps and chunks of stone sticking out of the sand and shingle. They are actually wooden pilings and stone supports that once formed part of the Royal Suspension Chain Pier – Brighton's very first pier.

Simply known throughout history as the Chain Pier, it was designed and constructed by Sir Samuel Brown. Completed in 1823 at a cost of £30,000, it was 352 metres long and 4 metres wide. The name came from its design, which consisted of a series of chain-like segments linked by tall suspension towers, like those more commonly seen on suspension bridges.

Although there were a handful of attractions on it such as a camera obscura, it wasn't built for entertainment, but to cope with an increase of cross-Channel traffic to the south coast after the Napoleonic Wars, and to offer a better landing spot for cargo boats bringing goods to the area.

In the 1840s, the railway finally came to Brighton. As a consequence, deliveries to the Chain Pier dwindled. Shipping business at the pier started to disappear, and with the building of the West Pier in 1866 specifically as an entertainment and shopping venue, the Chain Pier had outlived its usefulness.

By now, most of the pier had fallen victim to bad weather. Various bits of it had been swept away at one point or other; the remainder was washed away for good in a huge storm in 1896.

Today, the only remains of the once magnificent pier structure are what you see reappearing at very low tide.

Other vestiges of the Chain Pier

As well as these structural remains, a signal cannon and the Chain Pier's two original entrance kiosks (which once sat on the shore) survive. You'll find them close to the main amusement arcade on the Brighton Palace Pier (see p. 30).

A tablet commemorating the Chain Pier was put up on the wall along Max Miller Walk, exactly opposite its original site, but it has now disappeared. However, a plaque commemorating its designer and engineer, Sir Samuel Brown, can be found outside his former home at 48 Marine Parade, a beautiful Regency building now called Chain Pier House.

ATHINA-B ANCHOR

The legacy of an impressive wreckage in 1980

Madeira Drive, Brighton BN2

Opposite the start of the Victorian terraces at the western end of Madeira Drive, the anchor on a plinth once belonged to the *Athina-B*. This Greek merchant ship, which set sail on 11 December 1979 from the Azores loaded with tonnes of pumice bound for Shoreham, ended up as Brighton's most popular temporary tourist attraction.

The story goes that when the *Athina-B* arrived at Shoreham on 20 January 1980, gale force 8 winds prevented it from entering the harbour. As it hovered outside waiting to dock, the ship's engine failed and it started to drift towards Brighton, narrowly missing the pier before hitting a concrete groyne and tearing a hole in its hull.

The Shoreham Lifeboat Association rescued the entire crew, including the captain and his family, during several missions. Once everyone was safely back on land, the ship carried on drifting, finally running aground on the beach below Lower Rock Gardens.

In the month it took to organise moving her, the floating wreck became one of Brighton's biggest tourist attractions: thousands of people flocked to the seafront to see the giant vessel beached in the surf. Parties of schoolchildren were taken on day trips, artists arrived to capture the spectacular scene, and it's even thought that Volk's Electric Railway (see p. 40) ran an out-of-season service to provide curious visitors with a good view.

The ship was eventually hauled off the beach some time in February 1980 and was apparently taken to a scrapyard near Rainham. The anchor was returned to Brighton as a memento and placed where it now stands on the Madeira Drive promenade, together with a plaque marking the event and the successful rescue of the crew without loss of life.

The *Athina-B* is just one of many ships to have run aground on Brighton beach. Another was the *Atlantique*, which was wrecked on the Albion groyne on the night of 2 June 1860, with the death of one man.

A painting of the *Athina-B* by Dennis Roxby Bott is in Brighton Museum, although it's in storage and not currently on view.

FLINT GROTTO

An unofficial sculpture garden on the beach

Halfway between the Brighton Palace Pier and the Madeira Lift
Madeira Drive, Brighton BN2

What began as a simple and practical DIY project for Rory McCormack, a Brightonian described as the "last fisherman", has grown into a bizarre art project most people mistake for a neglected fenced-off enclosure full of old rubbish and fishing equipment.

Rory moved to Brighton with his family in the 1960s when he was just 5 years old, began fishing off Brighton beach as young as 16, and has held his fisherman's plot for 15 years. Fed up with cutting up fish and repairing his nets on the floor, he used his dry-walling skills to build himself a workbench out of material available along the beach: the flint pebbles and shells.

The project quickly snowballed and soon the workbench was decorated with nautilus and conch shells that Rory had gathered over the years. "I thought it was a good way to make use of some of the stuff that I had just lying about at home," he says.

Rory's original workbench is now just a small part of a much larger collection of ornate flint sculptures crammed into the tiny spaces in between his fishing equipment and the vegetable patch inside his plot. They can be seen clearly from the Volk's Electric Railway tracks and Madeira Drive as you look out to sea.

To date, Rory has created some eight larger-than-life sculptures, all with a robust and quirky appearance. Some have a link to ancient mythology while others are inspired by Bronze and Iron Age art. The most recent additions are a sculpture inspired by the Venus of Willendorf (dating from between 28,000 and 25,000 bce and considered one of the world's oldest and most famous surviving artworks) and a work representing a Sumerian goddess cradling a child. These are both smaller than the others so that, if necessary, they can be moved. There are also little non-figurative sculptures, such as a grave containing a skeleton, a throne and an entryway.

Rory began creating his sculptures without asking permission, which has led to his work being called "outsider art". In 2015, Brighton & Hove City Council described the site as a health and safety risk and told Rory to take it down: the future of this quirky "unofficial sculpture garden" now hangs in the balance.

MADEIRA LIFT

Old-fashioned fun

Marine Parade, Brighton BN2 1EN
Open throughout spring and summer from Easter
Admission free

Few people know that, for some novel entertainment, you can enjoy a free ride in the Madeira Lift, a Grade II-listed Victorian architectural gem restored to its former glory in 2013.

The lift was built at the same time as the huge Marine Terrace sea wall in around 1830 to link Marine Parade with a shelter hall below on Madeira Drive, designed to accommodate visitors in bad weather. Today, this hall is home to the Concorde 2 nightclub, which operates the lift on behalf of Brighton & Hove City Council.

In its heyday, the lift carried thousands of Victorians, dressed up in their seaside finery, from grand whitewashed Regency homes down to the beach for their daily constitutional.

It was originally operated using a hydraulic pump; up to 15 people could be carried at any one time for a halfpenny each way. Today, it's powered by electricity and carries only six people for free. You can ride up and down as many times as you like – an irresistible set-up.

Made out of cast iron, the lift was designed to resemble the oriental design of the Royal Pavilion and has four griffins and an ornate dolphin weather vane on the top. The original lift cage was decorated with mirrors, gilt panels and medallions, and had a glass roof.

As part of an intricate restoration project, the entire Madeira Lift was rebuilt in several stages, over a period of just under 10 years.

MAGNUS VOLK'S FORMER OFFICE AND WORKSHOP

The clubhouse of an eccentric inventor

Volk's Electric Railway, 285 Madeira Drive, Brighton BN2 1EN
www.volkselectricrailway.co.uk
Can be viewed from the outside only

Describing Volk's Electric Railway which opened along Brighton seafront in August 1883, and still functions today, *The Daily Telegraph* said: "A very interesting practical application of electricity".

Named after its eccentric creator, Mr Magnus Volk, the entrepreneurial and creative son of a German clockmaker – and today considered one of the greatest Brightonians – it's the first public electric railway of its kind in the country. It's powered using a 50-volt generator used by the madcap German inventor to light his own house in Preston Road.

The railway is a popular tourist attraction, but what's not widely known is that the two intriguing yet bizarre wooden buildings set into the cliff at Paston Place were where Volk set up his offices and workshop. And although they might look neglected, they're actually used by Volk's Electric Railway staff for their office and as a storage facility.

Inside, it's like stepping back in time: the rooms are decorated in traditional Volk's Electric Railway colours, the walls are lined with chocolate-and-cream painted wainscoting, and the store is jam-packed with all kinds of spare parts and wonderful old power tools. There's even a lump of metal from one of the Red Arrows' jets, which crashed in 1980 after clipping a yacht mast and a secret tunnel.

The larger building, known as "the arch", is thought to have been built to house a pumping station used to send seawater up to the local hospital – bathing in seawater was believed to aid a speedy recovery. However, it was never successful, so was used by local boatmen before Volk took out a lease on it and converted it into an office and workshop.

The smaller building, known as "the cave", was used as a generating station for the ill-fated Daddy Long Legs (see p. 278) before becoming another workshop and store.

It's thought that Volk liked to stand on the balcony and could often be seen there, keeping an eye on his drivers as they negotiated the viaduct.

In its early days, the railway was a luxurious affair, with one open car for twelve passengers, complete with mahogany sides and blue velvet curtains.

MADEIRA DRIVE GREEN WALL

The longest green wall in Britain

Madeira Drive, Brighton BN1

In Brighton's Madeira Terrace heyday, around the turn of the 19th century, it was billed on posters as "the world-famous sheltered walk", along which tourists and locals could promenade, unbothered by direct sunlight or rain.

What is now the Concorde 2 music venue on Madeira Drive was once an elegant tearoom, connected to the road above by a hydraulically powered lift – which is still in operation today (see p. 38). The terrace, with its beautifully latticed arches adorned with figures of Neptune and Aphrodite, was flanked by a series of ornate gardens and a boating lake.

Volk's Electric Railway ran beside it in places, and all along the cliff face was the remarkable Green Wall. Originally planted between 1870 and 1882, it decorated the entirety of the rendered cliff wall, helping it become one of the country's most elegant tourist destinations.

Today, it's considered the oldest green wall of its kind in the country and the longest – it stands 20-metres-high and is 1.2 km long. Classed as a Site of Nature Conservation Interest, the ecological equivalent of a listed building, it's also the only site of its kind in the UK.

Remarkably, the wall still thrives today and features around 100 plant species, including cow parsley, which grows mostly through March and June, foxglove, which blooms in mid-summer, a fig tree, plenty of ferns, and something called hoary stock, a coastal plant common on the south coast. One of the major features of the wall is a display of Japanese spindle, which still thrives even though it was established in the 19th century when the wall was first built.

Much of the work to protect the heritage of the Green Wall has been instigated by Brighton local, James Farrell, founder of a community organisation called Brighton & Hove Building Green. He works with volunteers and Brighton & Hove City Council to manage the section of the wall that runs from Madeira Drive up to Marine Parade. James organises "Green Gym" work parties twice a year, to help keep the wall in the best possible condition. There are future plans to restore it to its original extent. To find out more about the Building Green and the Green Wall, and to get involved, visit www.building-green.org.uk

BLACKROCK SUBWAY STUDIOS

A recording studio in a former toilet block

1 Black Rock Subway, Madeira Drive, Brighton BN2 5ZH
Tel: 01273 624435
www.blackrocksubway.co.uk
Open: Mon–Sun 9am–midnight. Occasionally open 24 hours

A curious doorway set into the Madeira Terrace wall near the Concorde 2 nightclub marks the former entrance to Studio 284, a once thriving rehearsal and recording venue with an unusual location – in a former gentlemen's toilet block.

"The toilet dates back to the 1950s and 60s and was 'frequented', I believe, by Quentin Crisp," says studio owner, Austen Gayton, "although the building itself dates back to the early 19th century, when it was a tunnel through which Victorian bathing carts were rolled into the sea. A surveyor once told me it was used as a laundry room for a hotel located where the Royal Crescent mansions are today – the towels and sheets travelled up and down on a dumb waiter in a shaft which you could still see behind the studio."

Austen opened Studio 284 at the end of the 1990s and it soon became a magnet for punk bands, which loved it for its special sound. It was a particular favourite with Brian James from The Damned, who moved to Brighton in the 1990s and recorded his solo album *The Guitar That Dripped Blood* here.

When the Victorian seafront terrace wall showed signs of being unsafe in 2015, Austen was forced to leave his much-loved long-term home. But it wasn't long before he opened a new venue called BlackRock Subway Studios just 500 metres further east along a subway tunnel near the old Black Rock swimming pool site – in yet another old toilet block.

The fact the new studio is in another loo is completely coincidental!" says Austen . "When I moved out of Studio 284, I had tons of equipment to store and the old Black Rock subway toilet block had just become free after 30-odd years. I ended up storing my equipment in it and it wasn't long before the penny dropped and the council offered me the option to relocate. So here I am, in yet another toilet!"

BlackRock Subway Studios officially opened in its new seafront subway toilet-block location in spring 2017. After a good clean-up and refurbishment, it now features two sound-insulated recording studios and a monitoring room.

Central Brighton

① WESTERN PAVILION — 48
② CONSTABLE'S FORMER HOME — 50
③ ANNA'S MUSEUM — 52
④ ST NICHOLAS REST GARDEN BURIAL VAULTS — 54
⑤ FRENCH PROTESTANT CHURCH — 56
⑥ "TWINS" SOUND-AND-LIGHT SCULPTURE — 58
⑦ "WRITE AROUND AIR STREET" ART STORY TRAIL — 60
⑧ TIME BALL — 62
⑨ FABRICA GALLERY — 64
⑩ BRIGHTON HIPPODROME — 66
⑪ MIDDLE STREET SYNAGOGUE — 68
⑫ OLD SHIP ASSEMBLY ROOMS — 70
⑬ THEATRE ROYAL BACKSTAGE TOURS — 72
⑭ MAX MILLER STATUE — 74

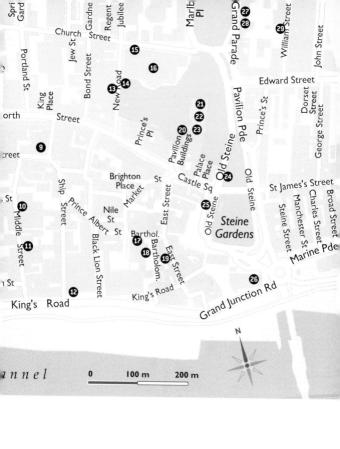

⑮	CERES SCULPTURE	76
⑯	BRIGHTON DOME BACKSTAGE TOURS	78
⑰	HENRY SOLOMON PLAQUE	80
⑱	OLD POLICE CELLS MUSEUM	82
⑲	QUADROPHENIA ALLEY	84
⑳	INDIA GATE	86
㉑	THE DRAWING CIRCUS	88
㉒	ROYAL PAVILION BASEMENT AND TUNNELS	90
㉓	PRINNY'S PIANO	92
㉔	ART DECO BUS SHELTER	94
㉕	FORMER HOME OF MARIA FITZHERBERT	96
㉖	DR RUSSELL PLAQUE	98
㉗	SCHOOL OF SCIENCE AND ART TERRACOTTA FRIEZES	100
㉘	UNIVERSITY OF BRIGHTON DESIGN ARCHIVES	102
㉙	WASTE HOUSE	104

WESTERN PAVILION

A miniature Royal Pavilion

9 Western Terrace, Brighton BN1 2LD
Can be viewed from the outside only

Next time you're shopping along Western Road, make a detour down the leafy side street of Western Terrace, where you'll find a building that looks uncannily like a miniature version of the Royal Pavilion.

This replica was no accident: built and designed between 1827 and 1828 by the well-known Regency architect Amon Henry Wilds as his own house, it intentionally resembles and pays homage to Brighton's most iconic landmark, including all its opulent oriental-style features.

The house combines Hindu, Orientalist and Indo-Saracenic styles, has two storeys and a basement and boasts a fascinating two-bay façade facing Western Terrace. The protruding entrance is set under a fancy archway below a parapet with an oriental-style balustrade.

According to historians Nicholas Antram and Richard Morrice in their Pevsner architectural guide to Brighton and Hove, the eclectic style "reveals Wilds' humour and his willingness to embrace the exotic".

Wilds died in 1857. In 1931 the Western Pavilion was converted into an office, before Debenhams bought it in 1957 and refronted the north façade facing Western Road with two-storey windows. They are still there today even though the house is a private residence once again. It was given Grade II-listed status on 13 October 1952.

NEARBY
Codrington Mansion

Back up on Western Road across the street, an old faded sign on a portico at 139 Western Road reads "Codrington Mansion". Royal Navy Commander Edward Codrington was hailed as a war hero when he destroyed the Turkish and Egyptian fleet at the Battle of Navarino (1827) during the Greek War of Independence. The sign refers to a terrace of houses he built and owned, known as Codrington Place. This includes his one-time home at Hampton Lodge around the corner, where he's said to have lived for four years. A blue plaque commemorating him and his time here was unveiled in 2009 at No. 140, a few doors along, by the Greek ambassador.

CONSTABLE'S FORMER HOME

A romantic great's seaside escape

11 Sillwood Road, Brighton BN1 2LF
Can be viewed from the outside only

One of the world's greatest painters, John Constable, lived in Brighton from 1824 to 1828, although it wasn't until recently that historians have managed to work out exactly where he and his family made their home.

Thanks to detailed, painstaking research by the Regency Society, the house has now been identified as 11 Sillwood Road. Although the outside has been altered, essentially the house is still the same inside as it was when the Constables lived in it. Today, it can be easily identified by a round blue plaque outside, marking the spot.

Constable decided to move to Brighton from London in the hope it would ease the symptoms of his wife's TB. During the four years they lived here, he created over 150 works of art, most of them inspired by the town, which was hailed by their guests – according to his wife, Maria – as "Hampstead with the addition of the sea". The painter is known to have enjoyed long, systematic walks in the surrounding area, which inspired many other works.

The key pieces of evidence used to track down Constable's former home were mostly found in letters between him and his good friend, Archdeacon Fisher, who lived in London. These revealed an address at 9 Mrs Sober's Gardens, and made reference to a neighbour called Mr Masquerier. He was a well-known portrait painter of the period, who bought 10 Sillwood Road from Mrs Sober in March 1824.

This information eventually led researchers to discover that Sober's Gardens was at one point renamed Sillwood Road. This turned out to be the place from which Constable wrote to Fisher, "I am looking for a month's quiet here and I have brought with me several works to complete. What a blessing it is thus to be able to carry one's profession with me."

Constable's Brighton walks: following in the great artist's footsteps

It's surprising how few people know that the great painter John Constable once lived in Brighton, let alone that he produced over 150 works while he was here.

In 2017, a critically acclaimed Brighton Museum exhibition, *Constable and Brighton*, saw 60 of the artist's sketches, drawings and paintings relating to his time in the city brought together for the first time. To coincide with the exhibition, the museum launched two circular Constable-themed walks around the city and surrounds, called *In Constable's Footsteps*.

The walks focus on the period that the artist lived in Brighton for his wife's health (between 1824 and 1828) and explore some of the places that inspired his paintings, including buildings he would have known.

The first walk is a 4-mile (6.4-km) city sightseeing tour, which begins at Brighton Museum in the Pavilion Gardens and takes between two and three hours. Sights include Constable's former home at 11 Sillwood Road (see p. 50); the school his children attended, run by his friend Henry Phillips; Little Preston Street, now believed to be the location of Constable's painting, *Houses at Hampstead*; St Ann's Well – Constable made many paintings from this viewpoint; Hove beach – the view west towards Shoreham was one of his favourite subjects; and the site of the Royal Suspension Chain Pier (see p. 32), the subject of one of the largest works to come out of Constable's time in Brighton.

The second walk, again starting outside Brighton Museum, explores places further out of the city centre that inspired Constable's work, such as West Blatchington Windmill (see p. 216); St Andrew's Church – restored since Constable sketched its ruins; Shoreham Beach; and Preston Park's elm trees (see p. 244). There's also the option to take a bus up to Devil's Dyke, one of the artist's favourite countryside spots, to witness the settings for more of his paintings, including those depicting the views over Shoreham.

Both walks are designed to be undertaken in your own time. Free guide leaflets are available from Brighton Museum and the Royal Pavilion, as well as Hove Museum (see p. 108), the Booth Museum of Natural History (see p. 246) and Preston Manor (see p. 230). They can also be downloaded from www.brightonmuseums.org.uk/constableswalks

ANNA'S MUSEUM

Taxidermy in a shop window

44 Upper North Street, Brighton BN1 3FH
www.annasmuseum.org
Can be viewed from the outside only

Anna's Museum isn't a museum in the traditional sense – it's an old Brighton shop window filled with curious pieces of natural history, geology and taxidermy. You can stop and look from the outside on an amble along the attractive Upper North Street.

The place belongs to young Brighton resident and natural history collector Anna Rubinstein, known around town as the city's youngest taxidermist. She started collecting things around age four, with her interest in taxidermy and natural history following a few years later.

By her teens, she had built up quite an array of natural history artefacts, which she displays as Anna's Museum. Everything is neatly presented in little wooden boxes and glass jars, all hand-labelled so you know what you're looking at.

Anna's fascinating collection grows and changes over time and includes things that animals leave behind, like antlers and teeth, wasps' nests and shed skin. There are also bits of bone and a few skulls, as well as pieces from far-away places – shells, fossils and rocks from the French-Italian border, precious stones, an earring from a tribe in Borneo and an arrangement of stone eggs.

At the time of writing, there was also a taxidermy frog, a large beetle,

a fox skin made from a dead animal that Anna found in the road, a curious stuffed squirrel in a bell jar holding an egg and wearing a waistcoat, a beautiful pheasant and a flying seagull, its wings outstretched, which Anna created during a workshop run by ethical taxidermist, Jazmine Miles-Long (www.jazminemileslong.com).

Such is the museum's appeal among fellow collectors and Brighton and Hove locals that Anna frequently receives regular donations. She always adds them to her display of treasures alongside handwritten letters from the donors.

Walk a little further west along Upper North Street, turn right just past The Windmill pub into Clifton Place and you'll discover the Clifton conservation area, home to some of the city's finest Regency and Victorian architecture.

ST NICHOLAS REST GARDEN BURIAL VAULTS

A leafy hidden gem

Dyke Road, Brighton BN1 3LJ

A few minutes' walk from the clock tower up Dyke Road is a grand stone arch and set of iron gates that mark the entrance to St Nicholas Rest Garden. This peaceful enclave was built as an extension cemetery to Brighton's parish church across the road in 1840 and is now a city park, offering a little breathing space from the busy shopping streets of Western Road.

If you visited here a few years ago, the chances are you wouldn't have seen its most unusual sight: a series of 14 burial vaults that were neglected and overgrown with ivy and knotweed until 2010. Today, the vaults have been unearthed and restored to their former glory.

A total of 23 vaults were originally planned as part of the famous Regency architect Amon Henry Wilds' grand vision for the extension rest garden, which included a burial pyramid with room for several thousand coffins and a castellated gatehouse. The pyramid proposal is thought to have been inspired by an astonishing design by an architect called Thomas Wilson for a similar cemetery planned for London's Primrose Hill with space for more than five million coffins. However, a change in public health legislation in 1854 – designed to prevent the spread of cholera and other contagious diseases –stopped the project in its tracks, which meant that only 14 burial vaults were actually built.

The vaults we see today are made from rubble and stucco and designed in a Tudor-Gothic style. They are real tombs and have big studded doors which look real, but aren't. Only vault 13 has a real wooden door.

According to The Mortiquarian, a useful website dedicated to St Nicholas Rest Garden, vault 13 with the real wooden door has never been occupied, perhaps due to associations with the unlucky number 13. Instead it's used as a tool store by the volunteer gardeners and is sometimes open for viewing or events. Visit the website: https://mortiquarian.com

A stroll around the rest garden reveals the graves of several notable people, including Sir Martin Archer Shee, a successful artist in the 1800s who went on to become President of the Royal Academy of Art from 1830 until 1845, when he was succeeded by Turner.

FRENCH PROTESTANT CHURCH

An architectural treasure

1A Queensbury Mews, Brighton BN1 2FE
Can be viewed from the outside only

In Brighton's Victorian seaside heyday, the town attracted a large crowd of overseas visitors, particularly from France, who helped to fill the pews in Brighton churches.

To ensure that these French visitors had a place to worship in their own language, Brighton resident Mrs E Hayes opened up her own house at 20 Montpelier Villas for such services, and made sure that a French-speaking vicar was available to preach.

Soon the congregation outgrew her home. Eventually, after many moves from one church to another, Mrs Hayes arranged for one to be built on a piece of land just off Regency Square, behind a row of houses that stretched from 121 King's Road to the corner of Regency Square.

On 27 February 1888, the French Protestant church was complete and consecrated for use in services (including a weekly Sunday service), marriages, funerals and christenings, which it celebrated for 120 years. By 2008, the congregation was dwindling, however, so the church committee decided to sell up and the building was finally deconsecrated.

Today, it's been converted into a charming private home. Unfortunately, the first owners stripped the property of the Victorian interior. Then two sensitive developers stepped in, taking far greater care to preserve this architectural gem, and going so far as to track down some of the missing fixtures and fittings, as much for the benefit of passers-by as for their own enjoyment.

The interior of the former church has been carefully turned into a delightful split-level home, which apparently has a stereo system tucked into the pulpit perched over an ornate porch entrance in the bedroom. It's also believed that the foundation stone has been turned and re-engraved with the original inscription.

NEARBY
The Queensbury Arms

Just opposite the church you'll notice a tiny pub on the corner. This gem of a drinking establishment was once known as the Hole in the Wall and claims to be Brighton's smallest pub.

Hidden history
It is said that a time capsule containing a newspaper, a bronze medal and a number of coins marking Queen Victoria's Golden Jubilee is concealed within the church's central foundation stone.

"TWINS" SOUND-AND-LIGHT SCULPTURE

Often seen but little understood

Churchill Square, Brighton BN1

Despite its dominating appearance, most people don't know that this futuristic-looking sculpture outside the Churchill Shopping Centre is a remarkable permanent sound-and-light installation – instead they opt to sit on it, mid-shopping spree.

Created by Brighton sculptor Charlie Hooker, *Twins* uses the passage of the sun across the sky to trigger sounds, which then emanate from the sculpture. The idea is that you sit on the ledge around the plinth and listen for these sounds that resonate when sunlight hits sensors on the sculpture – the sounds getting louder as the sun comes up and quieter when it goes down.

Each twin represents a pair of seasons – autumn and winter; spring and summer. They are made of four different types of coloured granite, each representing a season: Imperial Green for spring; Golden Summer for summer; Imperial Red for autumn; and Bethel White for winter. The plinth itself is carved out of standard grey granite.

Each granite surface has images etched onto bronze plaques: these come from weather pattern recordings taken on location outside the Churchill Centre at the time the sculpture was made in 1997. These patterns chart the sun's trajectory during the seasons and have been digitally translated into 12 pieces of music, one for every month of the year.

The idea for the piece was that the sounds made by *Twins* would draw people into Churchill Square. At night, a light shines from within the sculpture to produce two star shapes on the ground.

Charlie Hooker is Professor of Sculpture and Fine Art MA course leader at the University of Brighton. He has helped develop methods of teaching from primary education through to postgraduate level. His work over the past 30 years has ranged from music, performance and visual art to the producing of exhibitions, sculptures and installations that link art to science. For more information, visit www.charliehooker.co.uk.

"WRITE AROUND AIR STREET" ART STORY TRAIL

An exciting secret discovery

Air Street, Brighton BN1 3FB

Unbeknown to most busy shoppers dashing through Air Street, a tiny pedestrian thoroughfare that connects Queen's Road to Churchill Square, is an art installation so subtle it mostly goes unnoticed. But when you spot it, it makes for an exciting discovery.

So next time you're here, slow down and take the time to notice that subtly incorporated into the existing street furniture – a painted bollard at one end, a stainless steel bollard at the other, a brass plaque set into the ground, engraved paving stones and a cast-iron manhole cover – are five poems written by schoolchildren from the Brighton and Hove area.

Together, they form a public art story trail called "Write Around Air Street", a project initiated in October 2007 by the Children's Festival in conjunction with The South, a literary organisation which promotes writing and literacy skills for primary-school-age children.

To encourage engagement with the city's public spaces and improve literacy, children from Brighton and Hove schools aged 5 to 11 were invited to write a story or poem on the theme of "air", for the chance to have it included in the permanent story trail you see in the street.

The installation was launched at the Children's Festival in April 2008. It also included the work of 10 runners-up who had their work temporarily installed around the clock tower.

NEARBY
Clock Tower Cinema
The Quadrant Pub, 12-13 North Street, Brighton BN1 3GJ
Tel: 01273 733238
www.quadrant.pub
Opens at 8pm every other Monday
Free entry, free popcorn!

A few metres north of the clock tower (see p. 62), on your left as you head towards Brighton station, is one of Brighton's oldest pubs, which has a beautiful façade. As well as quenching the thirst of Brighton and Hove's busy shoppers and tourists for many years, the Quadrant is also home to a hidden screening room most people don't know is there. Called the Clock Tower Cinema, it shows classic cult movies twice a month on a Monday night, from *American Werewolf in London* to *Weird Science*, *The 39 Steps*, *The Breakfast Club* and *Blade Runner* – for free, with free popcorn thrown in.

TIME BALL

A timely occurrence

Brighton Clock Tower, Queen's Road, Brighton BN1 3GJ

ommissioned by local advertiser James Willing to commemorate Queen Victoria's Jubilee in 1887 and completed the following year, Brighton's Grade II-listed clock tower is a popular city landmark. It as a remarkable feature known as a "time ball" – a gilded copper ball on stick which rises hydraulically up the mast as every hour approaches nd then drops down again as the hour is struck. Originally, it was esigned so that passing ships could set their chronometers by it.

"It is highly likely that the Brighton time ball was dropped by means of telegraphic time signal that would have originated from the Shepherd gate lock at the Royal Observatory in Greenwich," says the Royal Observatory's urator of horology, Rory McEvoy. "Although most of these systems run om GPS or radio-controlled quartz clocks these days," he adds.

The Brighton time ball was created by the mad-cap German inventor Magnus Volk, of Volk's Electric Railway and Daddy Long Legs fame. It as turned off soon after its inauguration in 1888 because nearby residents omplained about the sound it made when the wind whistled through the ots up which the ball rose – this apparently scared the horses.

However, when the clock was refurbished in 2002, the mast and ball ere redesigned and the slots filled in to stop the noise.

The clock tower itself was designed by London architect John Johnson. lthough it has met with much criticism in the past – and even threats) demolish it – it remains one of the city's best-loved landmarks, second nly to the Royal Pavilion.

From 1852 to 1893, the Shepherd gate clock was at the heart of Britain's time system: its time was sent by telegraph wires to London, Edinburgh, Glasgow, Dublin, Belfast … and even to Harvard University in Cambridge, Massachusetts, via the new transatlantic submarine cable. It's considered one of the most important clocks ever made in terms of introducing accurate time into everyday life.

You'll find another example of a time ball on top of Flamsteed House at the Greenwich Royal Observatory. Its bright red ball is one of the world's earliest public time signals, distributing time to ships on the Thames and many Londoners. It was first used in 1833 and still operates today.

FABRICA GALLERY

A contemporary art gallery in a Regency church

40 Duke Street, Brighton BN1 1AG
Tel: 01273 778646
www.fabrica.org.uk
Open for temporary exhibitions and associated activities

Brighton is one of the country's art capitals, bursting with all kinds of little galleries and craft shops, but there's one that stands out from the crowd for its unusual setting. The former Brighton Trinity Chapel was built in 1817 by Amon Wilds for Thomas Read Kemp, the developer of Kemp Town. Today it's home to a contemporary art gallery called Fabrica.

The chapel closed in 1985 and became the temporary home for an exhibition on Brighton history. Meanwhile, a group of artists from Red Herring Studios established the Fabrica Gallery as a focus for contemporary visual art practice. With the support of South East Arts, Brighton Borough Council, the Foundation for Sport and the Arts and the Chichester Diocese, they opened in the space in 1996.

Nowadays, Fabrica hosts three main exhibitions a year, which are often developed in partnership with other cultural organisations in the local community, such as the Brighton Festival. Fabrica also commissions artists to make new work specific to the unique gallery space.

Alongside the exhibitions it hosts, the gallery organises a rich programme of supporting events and activities, including artist talks, screenings, drawing events, schools' workshops and artists in residence.

Perhaps the most special thing about an art exhibition at Fabrica is how well the contemporary works sit in contrast with the traditional interior of the chapel. It remains in good condition and includes a mezzanine balcony with lots of rich wood panelling, as well as a carved eagle lectern by a Mr Pepper of Brighton, who is said to have cast the Victoria Fountain dolphins.

A plaque on the outside wall of the church records the career of a successful and popular Brighton preacher at the church, Frederick W. Robertson. He had a significant impact on life in Brighton, undertaking missionary work in the town, founding a working men's institute and preaching radical, unorthodox but effective sermons that became famous throughout Britain.

Fabrica also participates in the annual Scalarama Film Festival, which hosts a series of pop-up films in unusual venues across the city every September. Visit https://scalarama.com/brighton/ for more information.

BRIGHTON HIPPODROME

The most important unused theatre in the UK

52 Middle Street, Brighton BN1 1AD
Currently closed. Can be viewed from the outside only

Middle Street isn't just home to "one of the most spectacular synagogue interiors in Europe" (see p. 68), it's also the location for its most intriguing abandoned building. Brighton Hippodrome has been dubbed "the most important unused theatre in the UK" by the Our Brighton Hippodrome campaign group, set up in 2016 by local volunteers concerned for its future.

Unfortunately, few people are allowed inside, but from the opposite side of the road, you can get a sense of its size and take a good look at its historical façade. The original signage can still be seen above the front canopies, as well as an impressive equestrian entrance– the only surviving example of its type in the UK – through which horses and other animals were once led to the side of the stage.

Brighton Hippodrome opened in 1897 as an ice rink, but was redesigned in 1901 for circus performances by the well-known English theatrical architect and designer, Frank Matcham. He included a stage with a proscenium arch and the animal entrance, hidden behind curtains on either side of the stage. In 1902, one of Matcham's students called Bertie Crewe redesigned it again, this time as a variety theatre. Crewe extended the stage into the auditorium and added an orchestra pit in front, filling the former circus arena with seats and introducing the elaborate and detailed ceiling that has been widely documented.

At one time, Brighton Hippodrome was the town's main theatre, hosting stars of the variety circuit such as Brighton-born Max Miller (see pp. 74 and 190), before it was extended in 1937 to create an auditorium seating 1,400. It wasn't long before the popularity of variety shows started to decline, however, which led to the venue shifting its focus to concerts and one-off special performances.

In October 1964, gigs by the Rolling Stones and the Beatles attracted full-capacity audiences of 4,000, but the theatre nevertheless closed the following year. After a brief stint as a TV studio, it became a bingo hall in 1967. It finally closed 40 years later in 2007, after being given Grade II* listing in 1980.

Shortly after the Hippodrome shut down, a proposal emerged to turn it into an eight-screen multiplex cinema. However, the ongoing local conservation campaign aims to ensure that the building remains a live theatre venue.

MIDDLE STREET SYNAGOGUE

One of the most spectacular synagogue interiors in Europe

39 Middle Street, Brighton BN1 1AL
www.bhhc-shul.org/middlestreet/
Open by appointment only and during the Brighton Fringe Festival in May each year

It's easy to walk past the Middle Street synagogue, see the boarded-up windows and assume it's closed to the public or has been abandoned. However, this striking building, tucked away up a humble seafront side street, is described by historian, conservationist and Regency Society founder Dr Antony Dale as having "one of the most spectacular synagogue interiors in Europe". Historic England has also named it among the top 10 most beautiful synagogues in the country.

Behind its steely Byzantine-style façade is a spectacular Grade II*-listed interior, largely unchanged since 1915. You can explore and learn more about the building on a private tour, or when it opens for the Brighton Fringe Festival.

The synagogue opened in 1875 to meet the needs of Brighton's expanding Jewish population, provide a new community focal point – there was once a schoolhouse behind the main building – and serve the illustrious Goldsmid, Rothschild and Sassoon families when they visited the coast.

Designed by local architect Thomas Lainson, it was originally fairly plain inside – even partly undecorated – but, between 1880 and 1915, donations from the Sassoons and the Rothschilds gradually furnished it with wrought iron, brass work and stained-glass windows. The lectern set in the middle of the gallery was presented by Albert Sassoon in 1887 to mark his son Edward's marriage to Aline de Rothschild. Two stunning menorah candlesticks on either side of the lectern were donated by Baroness Mayer de Rothschild and her daughter, Hannah.

The main feature of the interior is the spectacular ark at the eastern end of the synagogue. The scrolls are kept here behind ornate gates installed in 1915 – these replaced the originals you now walk through as you enter the main hall.

Unfortunately, the Middle Street synagogue has never attracted a particularly large congregation, for various reasons, including its location. It has been mostly closed since 2004, but opens occasionally for worship and special services.

The Sassoon family's interest in domestic electricity almost certainly resulted in the installation of electric lighting here in 1892, making Middle Street the first synagogue in Britain to have it.

OLD SHIP ASSEMBLY ROOMS

A Grade II-listed function room inside Brighton's oldest hotel

Old Ship Hotel, King's Road, Brighton BN1 1NR
Tel: 01273 329001
www.oldshipbrighton.co.uk
Open by appointment only

Hotels are ten a penny in Brighton, but there's one that stands out from the crowd for its history. Not only is the Old Ship Hotel on Brighton seafront said to be the oldest in the city, it's also home to the Old Ship Assembly Rooms – the original sign of which still exists on the Ship Street side of the hotel.

"Assembly rooms were fashionable entertaining spaces in the 18th and 19th centuries," says local historian, Jackie Marsh-Hobbs. "They usually consisted of a main ballroom, a card room and sometimes a tea or supper room." At the Old Ship Hotel, the main ballroom is known as the Paganini Ballroom; the Regency Suite is the former card room.

The Paganini Ballroom has Grade II-listed status and is the most well-known of the assembly rooms. It was remodelled out of the site of the original Tudor hotel, which records show first opened in 1559 as the Shippe Inn. Its spectacular interior features a balcony for spectators at one end and a carved musicians' gallery with delicate ironwork railings in the centre.

The room is named after the celebrated Italian violinist Niccolò Paganini, who once played from the balcony and stayed the night at the hotel. In 2009, the room was refurbished in preparation for the hotel's 450th birthday celebrations that year.

The Old Ship Assembly Rooms' development caught the attention of King George IV, who first visited Brighton in 1787. With his encouragement – if not his money – a gracious retiring room for the royal guest was added overlooking Ship Street. It is known today as the Gresham Suite.

An old-style lift said to be the prototype for those used on the *Titanic*

A wander around the hotel reveals several intriguing artefacts. These include a green leather armchair said to belong to Winston Churchill (see p. 120); an old-style lift believed to be the prototype for those used on the *Titanic*; and a commemorative plate from the Brighton Veteran Car Club, which had its first meeting in the hotel lobby.

Charles Dickens is said to have given a reading in the Paganini Ballroom in 1841. His rival, William Thackeray, is said to have stayed at the Old Ship Inn and used it as a location in his novel, *Vanity Fair*.

The hotel boasts a private dining room and bar set into smugglers' tunnels under the hotel (see p. 293).

THEATRE ROYAL BACKSTAGE TOURS

Behind the scenes at the city's oldest theatre

New Road, Brighton BN1 1SD
www.atgtickets.com/venues/theatre-royal-brighton/
Open for tours every Saturday at 11.30am

Originally opened in 1760 in a converted barn on the Old Steine, the Theatre Royal is today considered one of the oldest and most distinguished theatres in the country. It moved to Duke Street (before relocating to its current New Road address) when a Mr Hewitt Cobb bought it and schmoozed its most distinguished customer, the Prince Regent, to buy land opposite the Pavilion, in a bid to boost its profile.

Its fortunes fluctuated over the years under various owners, hitting a peak when a Mr Henry Nye Chart bought it and extended it. His wife – one of the first female theatre managers – took over when he died, continuing the theatre's success.

Although the Theatre Royal once hosted its own performances, today it's a touring venue, presenting shows from the West End or previews on their way to London, including ballet, music, comedy, opera and children's shows.

Among the stars who have graced its stage, and loved the theatre's compact size, are the Redgraves, Laurence Olivier, John Gielgud, Marlene Dietrich, Margot Fonteyn, Rex Harrison, Dame Judi Dench, Sir Ian McKellen and Patrick Stewart.

However, despite its rich heritage and star-studded ensembles, few visitors take advantage of the backstage tours: guides will take you behind the scenes, often jostling with props or with lighting and sound technicians preparing for matinees and evening performances. You are led through a maze of backstage corridors, studios and dressing rooms to the stage-door reception, where staff work their magic.

You'll also discover rare backstage features, such as a late 19th-century safety curtain counterweight and hemp ropes, and a scene-painting room, as well as a secret outside corridor. You'll learn the fascinating history of the Grade II-listed theatre we see today, redesigned in 1806 by prolific theatre architect Charles J. Phipps, who went on to design the Savoy, the London Palladium, the Lyric and the Garrick theatres.

Marlene Dietrich liked to relax by scrubbing the floor …

Nothing can make the star dressing rooms luxurious, but when Marlene Dietrich arrived in 1966, she immediately asked for a scrubbing brush to be brought to her room. It turned out that this was for purely recreational use – one of the greatest stars of the 20th century habitually relaxed before a performance by scrubbing the dressing room floor.

MAX MILLER STATUE

A memorial to Britain's original variety performer

Pavilion Gardens, New Road, Brighton BN1 IUG

As you enter the Pavilion Gardens from New Road, you'll notice a life-like bronze statue of a cheery-looking man to the left of the path. Hidden in plain sight amid the shrubbery, this is a memorial to Brighton-born showman Max Miller, who became Britain's most popular and highest-paid variety entertainer during the 1930s, 40s and 50s. Even today, fans still consider him the greatest stand-up comedian that Britain has ever produced.

The £30,000 bronze statue sculpted by Peter Webster (see also Steve Ovett's Foot, p. 252) was unveiled in 2005 in North Street before an audience of veteran show-business stars, including Norman Wisdom, June Whitfield, George Melly and Roy Hudd, alongside the Mayor of Brighton & Hove. Two years later, the statue was moved to the Pavilion Gardens.

Born in November 1894 at 43 Hereford Street in Brighton to a poor family, Miller's real name was Thomas Henry Sargent. Before he found fame, it's said he worked as a milkman, tailor, golf caddy and motor mechanic, and sang in pubs with his dad in the early 1900s. After the First World War, he began his professional career as a stand-up comic. He went on to develop his well-known "Cheeky Chappie" alter ego (inspired by his wife's nickname for him), which came complete with flamboyant multicoloured silk jackets and saucy gags.

Miller made films, toured in revues, and sang and recorded songs, some of which he wrote. He was best known for his intimate banter-style comedy, thought to be inspired by the Brighton seafront market-stall traders.

Miller lived in Brighton all his life at various addresses, including 160 Marine Parade (which he donated to St Dunstan's Hospital to use in the Second World War), Woodingdean House, Ashcroft in Shoreham, then 25 Burlington Street, where he died.

In 1999, several die-hard Max Miller fans got together to start the Max Miller Appreciation Society, which has Roy Hudd as president and Sir Ken Dodd and Michael Aspel as patrons. The society keeps the memory of Miller alive in various ways (for example, the erection of his statue), as well as social evenings, collecting memorabilia, publishing books and selling merchandise at www.maxmiller.org. A blue plaque to Miller was unveiled at his former home at 160 Marine Parade by Hudd and Aspel on 19 November 2006. Aspel also opened the Max Miller Room of exhibits and memorabilia at Bardsley's of Baker Street fish and chip shop in 2009 (see p. 190).

CERES SCULPTURE

Art overhead ...

Brighton Dome, Church Street entrance, Brighton BN1 IUE

The crowds of visitors queuing for gigs outside Brighton Dome each night barely spare an upward glance for the magnificent ceramic relief sculpture set into the arch above one of the entrances.

So next time you're waiting in line outside the Corn Exchange entrance near New Road to see a show, step back from underneath the canopy and look up: above it, you'll discover a beautiful piece of sculptural art hidden in plain sight.

This colourful mythological scene measures around 2 metres wide and 1 metre high and was created out of terracotta by the prolific British artist and sculptor, James Woodford. Designed to reflect the building's former heritage as a corn exchange, the work depicts Ceres, the Greek goddess of agriculture, standing in a serene pose, her hands out and head bowed, with three trumpeting angels on either side of her, floating on white clouds against a bright blue sky.

The sculpture was installed above the entrance and lobby designed by Robert Atkinson as an addition to the building in 1934.

Woodford studied at Nottingham School of Art and the Royal College of Art. His work includes a 3-tonne set of doors for the RIBA (Royal Institute of British Architects) headquarters in London, carved wooden screens for the RMS *Queen Mary* and a bronze statue of Robin Hood, which stands by the gates of Nottingham Castle.

The turquoise and pale green interlocking tiles that decorate the inside walls of the entrance are known as the Jackfield design. They were made by a company called Craven Dunnill, but designed and installed by the architect G Harold Elphick in 1906. These same tiles also decorate the Elphick-designed New Broad Street Turkish Baths in Spitalfields, London.

The Brighton Dome Corn Exchange was originally built as a riding school for the Prince Regent in 1808, adjoining the stables formerly located in what's now the Brighton Dome concert hall (see p. 78); both formed part of the Royal Pavilion Estate. The riding school was renamed the Corn Exchange on 1 October 1868, when Brighton's corn market moved here from its original home at the King & Queen Inn (which is still open for business as a pub around the corner in Marlborough Street). The Corn Exchange has also been used as assembly halls and as a military hospital during the First World War, before becoming the concert hall it is today.

BRIGHTON DOME
BACKSTAGE TOURS

From housing horses to hosting world-class acts ...

Church Street, Brighton BN1 1UE
Tel: 01273 709709
www.brightondome.org/about/history_heritage/tours/
Open for tours several times a year

When the glass-domed roof of the Prince Regent's new riding stables was complete in 1806, architect William Porden announced: "The cupola is now on, and the workmen are swarming about it like jackdaws ... the dome now supports itself without assistance from the scaffolding, and has not yet fallen!"

At 24 metres in diameter and standing 20-metres-high, this epic design inspired by the Corn Market in Paris was, at the time, one of the largest construction projects of its type in the world. Many people, upon seeing it being built, thought it would collapse once the scaffolding was removed. It didn't.

Today, the building is a renowned concert hall and hosts various shows, from standing music gigs to seated talks and theatre performances, as well as backstage tours led by informative guides who take you behind the scenes, through the warren of backstage corridors and underground tunnels. Depending what's happening on that particular day, you might even catch a glimpse of a band crew setting up or an orchestra warming up.

Tours begin in the concert hall with a fascinating historical introduction and the chance to learn about the original building. As you take in the size of the dome, it's crazy to imagine it was once made of intricate glass panels and hung with chandeliers, and that a roof so ornate was used to cover a stable building ... although the Prince Regent's taste for flamboyant fashions, outlandish architecture and mistresses is well documented.

The building was transformed into a concert hall in the mid-1800s, although the venue we recognise today, including the Art Deco styling, is the work of architect Robert Atkinson. A further major renovation in 1999 added cutting-edge technology, including removable stalls that slide into the orchestra pit to house a standing audience or extended stage, as well as an upgraded acoustic system.

A hidden historical instrument

Most people watching a show in the concert hall are unaware of the gigantic historic pipe organ that lies hidden underneath the stage. It dates back to the 1930s and thunders into action twice a year for the Brighton Dome Organ Showcase – an intriguing and little-known event in itself on the Dome's action-packed schedule. It was made bespoke by Hill, Norman & Beard in the 1930s, has 42 rows of pipes and four keyboards, and can produce a massive range of special effects, such as orchestral bells, marimba, harp, bird whistles and sleigh bells.

HENRY SOLOMON PLAQUE

Reminder of a remarkable character

Brighton Town Hall, Bartholomew Square, Brighton BN1 1JA

Outside Brighton Town Hall is a blue plaque that marks a gruesome and tragic event in the city's history, and is an important reminder of a man who spent his life working to make a difference in the community.

The plaque honours Henry Solomon, a prominent Jew and Brighton's first chief of police, who was bludgeoned to death with a poker in 1844 aged 49 while interviewing 23-year-old John Lawrence for stealing a roll of carpet.

Reports suggest that Lawrence became agitated during this process and that Solomon asked him to sit by the fire for a few moments to gather his thoughts, when the youth impulsively grabbed a poker from the nearby hearth. Lawrence was later found guilty of murder at Lewes Assizes and publicly hanged at Horsham.

The local population held Solomon in high esteem, and his good character and standing within the community are well documented in the history books. He was originally a watchmaker by trade, but opted for a life of municipal service, and was appointed the first chief officer of Brighton Borough Police in May 1838, with a team of 31 officers under his command.

At the time, the incident was seen as a tragedy for Brighton, but sympathy for Solomon and his large family – he had nine children – extended beyond the town, thousands turning out to join the funeral procession. A public meeting raised more than £1,000 for his dependents, including a £50 donation from Queen Victoria.

Solomon is buried in the Florence Place Jewish Burial Ground (see p. 262) near the Round Hill area of Brighton, and his grave is considered the most notable in the cemetery. The inscription reads: "15 years chief officer of police of the town of Brighton who was brutally murdered while in the public discharge of the duties of his office on the 14th day of March 1844 in the fiftieth year of his age".

Henry Solomon's ghost reputedly haunts the basement of Brighton Town Hall, now home to the Old Police Cells Museum (see p. 82).

On the north-west corner of the Brighton Town Hall building is another blue plaque, unveiled in 1955 to mark the site of St Bartholomew's Chantry. This was the local branch of the Cluniac Priory of St Pancras in Lewes, burned down by the French in 1514.

OLD POLICE CELLS MUSEUM

An underground museum in Brighton's first police station

Brighton Town Hall, Bartholomew Square, Brighton BN1 1JA
Tel: 01273 291052
www.oldpolicecellsmuseum.org.uk
Open for pre-booked guided tours. Call the Town Hall reception to book
Admission by donation

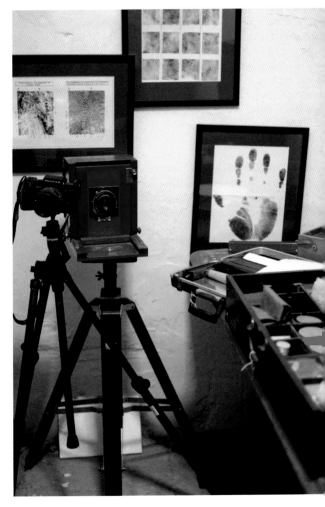

Hidden underground in the basement of Brighton Town Hall is the quirky Old Police Cells Museum. The city's first police station was established here in 1838 – originally at ground level until the pedestrian square was built at its current height. Its former parade room, offices and cells are now filled with memorabilia that tell the story of the history of policing in Sussex.

The walls are lined with nostalgic old pictures and cabinets packed with police-related objects, including uniforms and badges. There's also one of the largest collections of truncheons and tipstaves in the country – it was put together by Alderman Caffyn throughout his lifetime and is on permanent loan to the museum from the Sussex Police Authority.

Access to the museum is by appointment only. Visitors get an exhaustive tour with one of several enthusiastic tour guides, who start as far back as 700 years ago (when the Town Hall's current location was a market garden) and take you right up to the present day. You can feel what it's like to be locked up in a cell and also try on the various uniforms that date from the time the force began up to the present day.

Before Brighton's first police force was established, "watchmen" in top hats, armed with batons and rattles, patrolled the town. They were based at Brighton Town Hall until they were replaced in 1838 by the first police force: this consisted of a chief constable, two superintendents, a night constable, three inspectors and 24 constables, for a population of 47,000.

The force soon grew and by 1854 it had 10 officers and 51 constables. In the same year, it became the responsibility of the newly formed Brighton Borough Council, which further increased the size of the force by adding a police surgeon and a plain-clothes detective.

At the south-west end of The Level is a building that looks like a miniature house with a pitched roof and two chimney stacks. This curious structure was one of the city's first-ever "district" police stations – smaller police outposts that were opened up in various places around the town in the early days of policing in Brighton.

Sir Robert Peel founded the Metropolitan Police Force in London in 1829. Several members of the once prominent local Peel family are interred in the Peel Crypt underneath St George's Church in Kemptown (see p. 152), which the family owned for nearly 60 years in the 19th century.

QUADROPHENIA ALLEY

A hidden shrine to the mods

East Street, Brighton BN1 1HG

n May 1964, the nation was shocked by the violence that accompanied the country's first true youth culture. On the second May bank holiday weekend, thousands of mods and rockers descended on Brighton. It all nded in a mass fight on the beach, involving stones, deckchairs and waste bins being thrown and many people jailed.

Some say the media whipped up the conflict to create better headlines, but nevertheless, Brighton remains a favourite destination for bikers, rockers, mods and scooter boys during bank holiday weekends.

This part of Brighton's 1960s history was immortalised in the 1979 film *Quadrophenia*, set in Brighton and starring Phil Daniels, Ray Winstone, Sting and Leslie Ash, to name but a few. One of the film's best-known scenes, in which the two lovers escape the police and fall through doorway into a yard, was filmed in a hidden alleyway or "twitten" (see p. 172) just two minutes from the seafront.

Today, despite the fact that the alley is dingy, often smelly and covered in graffiti (weirdly, the doorway is still intact), it's become a shrine to the mods nd an unusual attraction nicknamed "Quadrophenia Alley": you'll find t tucked away between two clothes shops on the west side of East Street.

On the mod trail around Brighton

Lyn Daniels of Brighton Walks is a Blue Badge guide who offers bespoke *Quadrophenia* walks several times throughout the year. He also hosts a special bus tour every August bank holiday weekend (01273 302100; brightonwalks.com).

Hotel Pelirocco in Regency Square has its very own mod-themed room, complete with mod scooter bedside tables, called The Modrophenia (01273 327055; hotelpelirocco.co.uk).

For all your mod fashion needs, head to Jump the Gun (01273 626777; jumpthegun.co.uk) at 36 Gardner Street. You can follow this with refreshments in the mod memorabilia-filled Modern World Café Bar at 6–8 Madeira Drive on the seafront (01273 624382; www.modernworldcafebar.com).

Many of the mods and rockers jailed for fighting on Brighton beach were arrested and put into cells under Brighton Town Hall. These have since been turned into the quirky Old Police Cells Museum (see p. 82). You can still see some of the graffiti – initials and dates – that the mod and rocker prisoners scratched onto the walls.

INDIA GATE

An exotic entrance

Royal Pavilion Gardens, New Road, Brighton BN1 1UG

With its oriental-style domed design, it's easy to assume that this large Indian-style gate at the south entrance to the Pavilion Gardens is part of the original grounds. However, it was actually added much later, replacing an original gate erected by the Brighton Corporation – now Brighton & Hove City Council – after it bought the Pavilion from Queen Victoria in 1850.

Designed by Thomas Tyrwhitt in Gujarati style, the gate features a large dome resting on four pillars. It's often thought that it was paid for by public money, but it was actually a gesture of thanks from the people of India to the people of Brighton for the care "of her sons who – stricken in the Great War – were tended in the Pavilion in 1914 and 1915", and is dedicated to the inhabitants of Brighton.

During the First World War, several of Brighton's larger public buildings were used as "pop-up" military hospitals. Some 12,000 Indian Army soldiers, wounded while fighting with the Allied forces, were treated here between 1914 and 1915. These buildings included the Dome, the Corn Exchange and even the Royal Pavilion, where 4,300 patients were cared for in its 724 beds.

The York Place School (now part of City College's buildings) and the Kitchener Hospital (now Brighton General Hospital) – formerly the town's workhouse – were also used as military hospitals. These are recognised by the India Gate, even though they're not mentioned in the accompanying inscription.

The Maharajah of Patiala, Bhupinder Singh, unveiled India Gate on 26 October 1921. The maharajah was a great supporter of the British cause during the First World War and, in his speech, he reminded the crowds that he had sent 28,000 troops from his own state to fight in the war.

It is said he unlocked the gate with a gold key, claimed to be a replica of one of the original keys to the Royal Pavilion.

The Chattri monument – located on the fringes of Brighton near the area of Patcham – is another memorial commemorating India's relationship with Brighton during the First World War. It particularly honours the role played by the city's inhabitants in caring for wounded Indian soldiers. See p. 224.

THE DRAWING CIRCUS

Life-drawing classes with a difference

www.thedrawingcircus.co.uk
Open for various events: see website for details

There's nothing unusual about life-drawing classes. There are hundreds to choose from in this art-saturated city. But what if they were hosted by a troupe of theatrical performers and took place in unusual venues – after dark in the Booth Museum (see p. 246) or the Royal Pavilion, perhaps?

Introducing The Drawing Circus, a gang of Brighton-based artists, models, art tutors, musicians and performers who take on characters and lead innovative themed life-drawing events in unusual venues around Brighton, the south-east of England and beyond.

"We call our drawing circuses 'events' because they straddle the boundary between workshop and performance," says Drawing Circus co-director, Jake Spicer, who started the company in 2009 at the city's White Night Festival. "Our first event was so successful, we started preparing another one immediately – we've now run over 100."

The group draws much of its inspiration from 19th-century circus costumes, tempered with the characters of the performers and models that inhabit the costumes.

"It's as if we really have all run away with the circus," says Jake. "It's been fantastic to see the models take on their characters – after years working together, they've become more like us and we have become more like our characters. It's also exciting to see the drawings that come out of the events – the responses people make surprise and delight in equal measure."

Some events are put on in venues hired by the group, others are held in collaboration with specific venues such as the Booth Museum of Natural History (see p. 246), the Royal Pavilion, the Old Market (see Waterloo Street Arch entry, p. 126) or the Spiegeltent at the Brighton Fringe Festival. Others are commissioned by public bodies or colleagues in the arts, like teacher Emily Ball, who often hires the troupe to put on events for her students.

"The Pavilion has always been our dream venue since we started and we held our 100th Drawing Circus there in 2017," says Jake. "I'm not quite sure how we're going to top that!"

The collective also runs travelling drawing events from "The Cabinet of Wonder", a gypsy-caravan-like moveable stage which it has dragged through the Sussex woodlands, along the Hastings seafront and through the streets of London. It was inspired by 18th-century travelling *Wunderkammer*, cabinets of curiosity that were used to show off the wonders of the natural world.

ROYAL PAVILION BASEMENT AND TUNNELS

The secret underground world of a Brighton landmark

Royal Pavilion, 4/5 Pavilion Buildings, Brighton BN1 1EE
http://brightonmuseums.org.uk/royalpavilion/
Tel: 03000 290902
Tours take place every Thursday at 4.15pm and last 45 minutes

Brighton Pavilion is hardly a secret; however, the basement corridors and underground passageways beneath it have remained relatively unknown to the public until recently, only opening for tours in 2016.

Built as the seaside party palace for King George IV, the Pavilion is known for its exotic design, both inside and out, but beyond its splendid façade and entryways hidden behind velvet ropes lies an intriguing world.

A tour of the basement offers a behind-the-scenes peek into life below Brighton's most famous landmark. It encourages us to spare a thought for the 126 Pavilion staff who worked tirelessly in this secret underground world to keep the building running at full speed and dancing to King George's exuberant whims.

The basement and corridor system ran the length of the building and allow us to glimpse into the past – from how the staff worked to how the building was powered. It was designed to ensure that work appeared seamless, allowing servants to manoeuvre easily from one room to another without being seen, emerging as if by magic into various rooms up tiny secret stone staircases, before disappearing down them again.

Rooms with curious names – the foul linen store and band room – branch off the servants' corridors lined with original Dutch-glazed tiles. Overhead you can't fail to notice the complex series of pipes that formed the old steam-heating system – apparently so effective that guests were known to complain of the heat.

An old Victorian boiler too cumbersome to move remains in one of the underground rooms, while footprints of the Pavilion's original design can be seen in the form of an old bay window.

The tour ends with a visit to the 60-metre-long tunnel built later in 1821 connecting the Pavilion with King George's stables – now Brighton Dome (see p. 78). Although rumour has it that he used the passageway to meet his mistress, Maria Fitzherbert, the tunnel was actually built long after their relationship ended. It was designed to allow George to visit his horses without being seen by prying eyes.

Shafts in the stable tunnel's roof once held huge glass lanterns that emerged in the flowerbeds above, letting light into the tunnel. They've now been glazed over and can be seen on the ground outside when you exit the Brighton Museum & Art Gallery gift shop at the end of the tour.

PRINNY'S PIANO

A long-lost musical masterpiece

Royal Pavilion, 4/5 Pavilion Buildings, Brighton BN1 1EE
www.brightonmuseums.org.uk/royalpavilion/
Can be seen during museum opening hours: October–March 10am–5.15pm;
April–September 9.30am–5.45pm

When the Royal Pavilion was sold to Brighton in 1850, Queen Victoria stripped it of its contents, only to start returning them when she realised the building was not going to be demolished, a process which has continued under successive monarchs.

One of the items disposed of was a beautiful grand piano belonging to King George IV, which recently returned to its original Royal Pavilion home after it disappeared from the Royal Collection many years ago – no one knows exactly when. The piano still works, but has been dormant for 20 years and needs some restoration.

In 1821, George IV commissioned renowned piano-maker Thomas Tomkison to make the instrument for his Royal Pavilion home – it's now considered one of the most celebrated of Tomkison's surviving creations. He took a flamboyant approach to piano design, which is thought to have appealed to George's adventurous, francophile taste.

The piano is described as an elegant rosewood grand and is extravagantly decorated, inlaid with brass, gilt mouldings and turnbuckles, and with elegantly carved legs. It cost around £236, well over twice the price of a standard high-quality English grand piano at the time. Accounts also reveal that Tomkison supplied other "extra elegant" pianos to the Prince Regent, although none of them are known to have survived.

Brighton Museums bought the piano at auction for £62K with money it raised from the Art Fund, the Arts Council England/Victoria and Albert Museum Purchase Grant Fund, the Leche Trust and the Royal Pavilion Foundation.

Various paintings of the time show the piano on display in the Pavilion. Among them is a watercolour in a book called *Views of the Royal Pavilion at Brighton* (published in 1826) by Pavilion architect John Nash (pictured above). A reproduction of the painting is on display in the Royal Pavilion entrance hall.

Thomas Tomkison was one of the leading piano-makers of the late 18th and early 19th centuries. His fame was such that he attracted the patronage of George, Prince of Wales. In 1813, he acquired a royal warrant. Tomkison made a substantial fortune and amassed a considerable art collection, including works by his personal friend, William Turner.

ART DECO BUS SHELTER

A relic of Brighton's transport heyday

Old Steine Gardens, Brighton BN1 1NP

Brighton might have lost its tram system at the start of the Second World War, but you can still find a few relics of its road transport heyday hidden in plain sight in the Old Steine and Old Steine Gardens area. There are four Art Deco-style shelters, one of which has been used to protect tram and trolleybus – and now bus – users from the bad Brighton weather since the 1920s.

The earliest and perhaps the most impressive example is a Grade II-listed shelter near the Victoria Fountain on the western edge of Old Steine Gardens. It's also the largest of the four, and survives – albeit somewhat altered from the original – as the Gossip Café (pictured).

It's thought to have been built in 1926 by borough engineer, David Edwards, who used brick with a rendering of an odd-sounding material called "Brizolit" (a Czech patent of an artificial stone exterior finish with sparkling flecks of mica). The shelter was designed to reflect the Art Deco or Modern style of the time, which saw many buildings – particularly bus shelters – featuring rounded corners, long horizontal lines and smooth polished surfaces.

The other three shelters stand in a row in front of the Royal Pavilion. They're a lot smaller, yet look almost identical to the original. However, although Heritage England states that they were built at the same time as the first, John Blackwell, chairman of the Sussex Industrial Archaeology Society, has discovered that they are in fact replicas built around 30 years later, in the 1950s.

"If we look at the Brighton Land and Works Committee records dating back to 1949," he says, "the minutes from one of their meetings record that 'at Old Steine (between North Street and the Royal Pavilion) three stops built of traditional materials similar to the shelter and conveniences opposite Marlborough House are to be provided at an estimated cost of £1,350'. This means they definitely weren't built in 1926, but much later, although they were designed to replicate the original shelter as much as possible."

FORMER HOME OF MARIA FITZHERBERT

Brighton's own "Queen of Hearts"

Steine House, 55 Old Steine, Brighton BN1 1NX

An unusual white rectangular ceramic plaque outside what's now the YMCA building on the Old Steine alerts passers-by that Maria Fitzherbert once lived here.

Designed by Sussex sculptor Eric Gill, the plaque was unveiled in 1925. It says: "In this house lived Mrs Maria Fitzherbert from 1801 till her death in 1837." Originally located on the Steine Lane side of the building, it was apparently moved to its present site on the front in 1956.

Maria Fitzherbert is remembered as the "secret wife" or "illegal wife" of George, Prince of Wales (later George IV), whom she married in a secret ceremony in Park Street, London, on 15 December 1785 when she was 29 years old. However, without permission to marry from George's father, the union was deemed illegal under the Royal Marriage Act of 1722 and the Prince Regent was forced to distance himself from Maria.

George later reluctantly married his cousin, Princess Caroline of Brunswick, whom he didn't love and inevitably separated from, eventually resuming his relationship with Maria.

The couple never lived together although George had Steine House built for Maria conveniently close to his residence, the Royal Pavilion. She lived at Steine House until she died in 1837, surviving George by seven years. Maria was popular with the ordinary folk of Brighton, who genuinely mourned her when she died.

She is buried near the altar in St John the Baptist's Church, Bristol Road, East Brighton.

Steine House was designed and built by the Prince Regent's official architect, William Porden, who also designed the Prince's riding house and stables – now Brighton Dome (see p. 78). According to Rose Collis in *The New Encyclopedia of Brighton*, the original design featured an elaborate Egyptian-style colonnade. This was replaced with an Italian-style trellised verandah and balcony, supported by pillars, after it blew down in 1805. The house has been altered so many times over the years that, although it's listed, this is mainly for its historical associations rather than its architectural qualities.

Fewer than a quarter of the city's blue plaques pay tribute to women, although there is one – albeit not blue – which commemorates Maria Fitzherbert. It can be found outside St John the Baptist's Church in Kemptown, where she's buried.

DR RUSSELL PLAQUE

Remembering "Dr Brighton", the old man of the sea

Royal Albion Hotel, King's Road, Brighton BN1 1NT

Surprisingly, you have to look pretty hard to find this tribute to the man credited with creating the idea of Victorian seaside mania and reviving the fortunes of the impoverished fishing town of Brighton in the mid-18th century.

However, outside the Royal Albion Hotel, on Brighton seafront, a grey plaque reads: "On this site stood Russell House where lived from 1759 Richard Russell …"

As a small fishing town, Brighton had seen better days. However, when the idea of seaside resorts caught on in Victorian times, the place became a blueprint for such resorts around the world. Some people attribute this whole idea to one man, Dr Richard Russell, although, surprisingly, Brighton doesn't really shout about him.

Dr Russell wrote a book called *A Dissertation on the Curative Powers of Seawater* and, although he was by no means the first to recommend seawater as a cure, his work seemed to capture the public imagination. In 1753, Dr Russell moved from his home in Lewes to Brighton, built a house where the Royal Albion Hotel now stands, and set to work establishing all the new facilities that would be required in a resort intended for the wealthy. As a good networker with excellent political contacts, he also managed to enlist the help of various Sussex businessmen.

This, of course, attracted more doctors to Brighton's shores and, by the mid-18th century, the beach was filling up with that other great object of the period - the bathing machine. This was to become an important source of new income for the fishing families.

It was at this point that tourism and the leisure industry really began. The people of Brighton were keen to move into tourism since the place had once been so poor. Brighton as a resort was taking off!

The Russell plaque also reads: "If you seek his monument look around." If this sounds familiar, that's because it was "borrowed" from the epitaph to Sir Christopher Wren inside St Paul's Cathedral in London.

Dr Richard Russell had a literary side-career as one of the editors of the *Grub-Street Journal*. This satire on popular journalism – a Georgian version of *Private Eye* – was published between 1730 and 1738.

SCHOOL OF SCIENCE AND ART TERRACOTTA FRIEZES

27

Hidden remnants of Brighton's original art school

University of Brighton Faculty of Arts, 58–67 Grand Parade, Brighton BN2 0JY
Tel: 01273 643217
www.arts.brighton.ac.uk
Open during term time 9am–7pm; holidays 9am–6pm
Closed between Christmas and New Year

Before the University of Brighton Faculty of Arts moved into its glassy modern Grand Parade premises, it occupied a beautiful terracotta building, remnants of which can be found in the foyer of its new home.

Enter through the main door: to the left of the reception on the wall above, and opposite the door to some stairs, you'll see two large relief sculptures, as well as four smaller ones on two pillars. Although these might look like works of art in their own right, they're actually panels from the main façade of the original 1877 building. They were designed by Alexander Fisher and manufactured by Messrs Johnson in Ditchling.

The new Brighton School of Science and Art was a grand Romanesque-style building with polished red granite columns flanking the main entrance, Bath stone coping and cornices, and a brick façade enriched by the series of terracotta panels and lunettes that can be seen today in the lobby.

The scenes on the two bigger panels were designed to symbolically represent the kind of activities that would take place at this new school. An article in the *Brighton Herald* dated 3 February 1877 describes them nicely: "… pottery is represented by a boy carrying an earthen vessel; architecture, by another constructing a toy-house; sculpture, by a sculptor at work on a bust; geometry, by a fourth figure examining a scroll; building construction, by a youth with a saw and a plank; painting, by an artist at his easel, and so on. It says much for the artistic genius of Mr Alexander Fisher, the head master, who furnished designs for the decorations, that appropriate emblems have been given to each of the various figures."

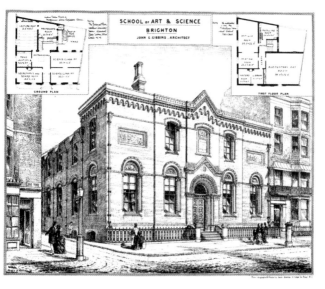

28

UNIVERSITY OF BRIGHTON DESIGN ARCHIVES

Underground collections

University of Brighton Faculty of Arts, 58–67 Grand Parade, Brighton BN2 0JY
Tel: 01273 643217
www.arts.brighton.ac.uk/collections/design-archives
Open by appointment only
Admission free

Hidden underneath Brighton University's main building on Grand Parade, in what was once the Basement Club, is an extensive collection of 20 design archives that constitute an internationally significant research base for scholars and students. Two of the archives relate directly to the history of Brighton itself.

The first is the Brighton School of Art Archive, which tells the story of this remarkable artistic institution which was – believe it or not – established at first above the kitchen of the Royal Pavilion in January 1859, moving to its own building on Grand Parade in 1877. When it eventually outgrew this building, it was forced to move into larger, more modern premises on the same site in 1961. The archive comprises photographs, curricula and other records that document the activities of staff and students throughout the school's long history.

The second, the Vokins Archive, tells the story of Brighton's longest-standing, although somewhat lesser-known, department store called Vokins. It was the mainstay of the Brighton retail scene for over 100 years until it closed in 1997.

The archive is a nostalgic treasure trove of records, including beautiful old photographs, carrier bags, documents, press cuttings, ledgers, plans, and correspondence relating to staff, sales, stock, store development and promotion.

Terracotta friezes

Before the University of Brighton Faculty of Arts moved into its glassy modern Grand Parade premises, it occupied a beautiful terracotta building, remnants of which can be found in the foyer of its new home (see p. 100).

WASTE HOUSE

29

The house that trash built

58-67 Grand Parade, Brighton BN2 0JY
http://arts.brighton.ac.uk/projects/wastehouse
Open as a pre-booked creative studio and events space

Just behind the University of Brighton's College of Arts and Humanities building, in the centre of Brighton, is this recycled home. The Waste House – as its name suggests – is made almost entirely from material thrown away or not wanted … the first structure of its kind in Europe.

The project is a collaboration between Duncan Baker-Brown, an architect and researcher with the College of Arts and Humanities, and Cat Fletcher, founder of the website Freegle, and creator of Brighton's City Waste Depot.

The Brighton Waste House aims to prove that undervalued so-called "waste material" has the potential to become a valuable resource and that there is therefore no such thing as waste, "just stuff in the wrong place".

It also aims to show that it's possible for a contemporary, innovative, low-energy building to be made almost entirely by young people studying construction trades, architecture and design.

Over 300 students worked on the project, which was fabricated in the workshops of City College Brighton and Hove, assembled and completed by students and apprentices between May 2013 and April 2014, and monitored by a PhD student from the Faculty of Science and Engineering.

Materials that have gone into the house include old vinyl banners you might see tied to lampposts to advertise gigs used as internal vapour control layers, waste bricks, sheets of plywood and off-cut timber from construction projects, as well as "rubbish" such as old plastic razors, denim jeans, DVDs and video cassettes. Old toothbrushes have even been used to insulate the wall cavities – the house has over 20,000 of them once used by business- and first-class passengers flying from Gatwick. There's also a rammed-earth wall made out of 10 tonnes of chalk waste consisting of 10 per cent clay, which is particularly good at storing passive solar energy.

Today, the house is a "live" research project: it's updated and monitored as part of the university's Sustainable Design MA course.

It's also used as a venue for creative workshops, seminars and events that are hosted or curated by artists, makers, designers, scientists, building contractors, or whoever wants to be involved in testing ideas related to sustainable design.

Central Hove

① JAIPUR GATE 108
② EVEREST'S GRAVE 110
③ ORNATE INTERIOR OF THE SACRED HEART CHURCH 112
④ THE HOVE CLUB 114
⑤ THE JUGGLER STATUE 115
⑥ 33 PALMEIRA MANSIONS 116

⑦ BODHISATTVA KADAMPA MEDITATION CENTRE 118
⑧ WINSTON CHURCHILL PLAQUE 120
⑨ THE REGENCY TOWN HOUSE 122
⑩ HEADLESS STATUE 124
⑪ WATERLOO STREET ARCH AND GARDEN 126
⑫ ST ANDREW'S CHURCH 128

JAIPUR GATE

An ornate gateway from the 1886 Colonial and Indian Exhibition in London

Hove Museum, 19 New Church Road, Hove BN3 4AB
Tel: 0300 029 0900
http://brightonmuseums.org.uk/hove/
Can be viewed from the outside 24/7

Visitors to the Hove Museum on New Church Road are met by an unusual, yet impressive gate-like structure that stands in the garden to the left of the path. It was originally commissioned by the Maharaja of Jaipur to mark the entrance to the Rajputana (now Rajasthan) section of the Colonial and Indian Exhibition held at South Kensington, London, in 1886. The exhibition was opened by Queen Victoria and attracted 5.5 million visitors during the three years it was open.

After the event, the gate was transferred to the Imperial Institute and eventually donated to the Hove Museum in 1926. It's not known why Hove was chosen as the benefactor, although many of the town's residents had links with India and retired to Hove after doing their stint for the Empire.

Although the Jaipur Gate was built as an entranceway, its design is in fact inspired by a type of bandstand that stood in the courtyards of Indian temples and palaces. Carved and assembled by Indian craftsmen, the gate was jointly designed by two Englishmen – Colonel Samuel Swinton Jacob and Surgeon-Major Thomas Holbein Hendley.

On the front is an inscription in gold lettering, in English, Sanskrit and Latin, showing the motto of the Maharajas of Jaipur: "Where virtue is, there is victory." It formed the backdrop for a later Maharaja of Jaipur's visit to Hove in 1986 to mark India's independence celebrations.

In 2004 the gate was dismantled for conservation, structural reinforcement and weatherproofing by specialist contractors. Resin repairs and reclaimed teak sourced in India have replaced decayed timber and a new copper dome and lead roof provides protection against rain.

Hove Museum's 11-ft-high (3.35 metres) iron gates have a wealth of history of their own, according to local historian, Judy Middleton, in her blog "Hove in the Past". They're thought have been made in the Georgian period by a Suffolk firm as gates for a manor house called Bramford Hall near Ipswich. In the 1950s, the Hove Art Collection Fund bought them for £250 as a memorial to Major Robert Woodhouse, a gifted craftsman who produced wrought-iron items for Hove Museum. However, it's not known why the fund chose these particular gates.

EVEREST'S GRAVE

Brighton's mystery guest, who gave his name to Mount Everest

St Andrew's Church, Church Road, Hove BN3 2FN
www.standrewshove.org

We're all familiar with Mount Everest in the Himalayan mountain range, the tallest mountain in the world. Perhaps less well known is the man it was named after, Sir George Everest, who just happens to be buried at St Andrew's Church in Hove – although his connection with Brighton or Hove, and why his family are buried at St Andrew's, remains a mystery.

A military engineer and geodesist, Everest went to India in 1823 to take on a mammoth task called the Great Trigonometrical Survey, a project that involved measuring the entire Indian subcontinent with great precision. The project was started in 1806 by British soldier, surveyor, and geographist Lieutenant-Colonel William Lambton.

The survey would take up 25 years of Everest's life and ended up mapping a huge area – almost 2,400 km – from Kanyakumari in the south, to the Himalayas in the north. Historical accounts suggest that Everest was relentless in his pursuit of accuracy and that he made countless adaptations to the surveying equipment, the methods and the calculations involved to get the best results.

Seven years after he was appointed superintendent of the Great Trigonometrical Survey, Everest was also made Surveyor General of India, with Mount Everest – which was originally named Peak XV of the Himalayas – renamed soon afterwards in honour of his pioneering mapping work. The Tibetans, however, still call it Chomolungma, meaning "Mother Goddess of the Earth", while the Nepalese refer to it as Sagarmatha, or "Goddess of the Sky".

Interestingly, it's thought that Everest never climbed the mountain. It's also alleged that there's no real evidence he even saw its summit, though it's known that he did travel to the foothills of the Himalayas as part of his work.

Everest retired in the mid-1800s and returned to England, dying 20 years later in London. He was buried shortly afterwards at St Andrew's Church in Hove and interred in the same grave as his two children, who had died in early childhood.

ORNATE INTERIOR OF THE SACRED HEART CHURCH

Don't forget to look up!

39 Norton Road, Hove BN3 3BF
Tel: 01273 735179
www.sacredhearthove.org.uk
Open: Mon, Tues and Thurs 9am–1pm, Wed and Fri 8am–9am,
Sat 5pm–7pm, Sun 9am–12.30pm. And at various times in May for
the Brighton Fringe Festival

Oscar Wilde's lover, Lord Alfred Bruce Douglas – nicknamed Bosie – is rumoured to have been received into the Catholic Church at the Sacred Heart. As well as this claim to fame, the church has one of the most magnificent interiors in the city, in addition to an impressive collection of artwork, sculptures, stained glass and frescoes – which you can see when the church opens its doors to the public for a few days during the Brighton Fringe Festival.

The Grade II-listed Church of the Sacred Heart is the oldest of Hove's three Roman Catholic churches and dates back to 1880. Inspired by the English Gothic style of the 14th century, it was designed by John Crawley, built in three stages and comprises a nave, sanctuary and isles. It was lengthened in 1887, and the cloister enlarged in 1911. The building opened in 1881 and was consecrated that same year, marked by 12 consecration crosses and brass sconces dotted around the church where the walls were anointed.

A nice way to explore the church's interior is to follow the self-guided art tour given out to visitors during the festival. Starting at the baptistery by the cloister entrance, it follows a route through the church designed to reflect the journey of Christian life towards the east end, the place of sunrise and symbol of eternal dawn, taking you to the sanctuary and the altar. This is where you'll see what's arguably the church's most impressive feature – a stunning vaulted ceiling covered in painted canvas panels that makes for a dramatic sight.

The panels were created by Nathaniel Westlake, a well-respected 19th-century British artist usually specialising in stained glass, who also designed some of the church's stained-glass windows. The panels depict God as the divine hand pointing to Jesus Christ and the Holy Spirit, the Virgin Mary receiving her crown at Christ's feet, seven archangels with St Joseph, St Joseph of Arimathea, St Stephen and St John the Baptist.

You'll find more murals by Nathaniel Westlake decorating the wall in front of the chancel arch in St John the Baptist Church in Bristol Road, Kemptown, where Maria Fitzherbert, the Prince Regent's mistress, is buried.

The church holds one mass a week in Latin and also broadcasts some of its services live on its website.

THE HOVE CLUB

An historic private members' club

28 Fourth Avenue, Hove BN3 2PJ
Tel: 01273 730872
www.thehoveclub.com
Open for members and their guests: Mon–Thurs 10am–8pm,
Fri 10am–10.30pm, Sat 11.30am–8pm, Sun 11.30am–4.30pm
Membership from £40 a month

On the corner of Fourth Avenue and Albany Mews is a striking classic Victorian red-brick building. This is the long-term home of The Hove Club, an exclusive members' club that's still going strong after it opened 127 years ago.

It was originally founded in 1882 as the Hove Reading Rooms in premises known as the Willett's building at the north-east corner of Grand Avenue. It opened as a place for Hove's important gentlemen – mainly of a military background – to gather together and socialise, read the papers and daily telegrams, chew the fat and play games including golf, billiards, whist, chess, bowls and croquet.

By the 1890s, the club had gained a solid reputation and an ever-increasing membership. This meant it had to move to bigger premises a couple of times before making this magnificent Grade-II listed Victorian building (commissioned for £5,882) its final home in 1898.

Today, membership is open to people from a wide range of professional and business backgrounds, not just the military. Ladies are now welcome to become full members, although previously the club was for men only. In the name of tradition, there's still a dress code, although slightly less formal than it once was.

Inside, it's a maze of little rooms set across two floors, all decorated traditionally, where members can come and relax. There's a snooker room, three function rooms, a reading and television room, a fine-dining members' restaurant, a bar and beautiful gardens.

NEARBY

The Juggler Statue ⑤
Hove Town Hall, Norton Road, Hove BN3 3BQ

Opposite Hove's longest-running institution The Hove Club, you can't miss the gargantuan 1970s brutalist building that is Hove Town Hall. Designed by John Wells-Thorpe (see p. 178) and completed in 1973, it sits in complete contrast to the rows of Victorian buildings surrounding it, as well as the unusual statue outside its front entrance – Hove's first new public artwork for 75 years at that time. This quirky 3-metre-high sculpture called *The Juggler* depicts a man pedalling on a unicycle and juggling with firebrands. Made of bronze with a blue-green patina, it's a replica of a piece by sculptor Helen Collis, a member of the Fiveways Artists group. It was presented to the Town Hall by her husband in December 1995.

33 PALMEIRA MANSIONS

*An exceptional example of Victorian
"nouveau riche" taste*

15 Church Lane, Hove BN3 2FA
www.elc-schools.com/about/elc-brighton/palmeira-mansions
*Open every weekday from 3pm for private tours; public tours take place in May
as part of the Brighton Fringe Festival*

At the north end of Palmeira Square across Church Road are two impressive south-facing terraces of grand Victorian properties. They were built between 1883 and 1884, and are almost identical: each four storeys high with an attic and basement, although one of them stands out from the crowd.

No. 33 Palmeira Mansions is not only unusual in that it's managed to remain a single building and avoid being split into flats; it also boasts a spectacular Grade II-listed interior that offers a fine example of Victorian "nouveau riche" taste. Many of the original features have miraculously survived the ravages of time and development.

Designed by local architect J. H. Lanchester and builder Jebez Reynolds Jr, the house was bought by a Mr Gillespie. He sold it not long afterwards in 1889 to a wealthy businessman, Mr Arthur William Mason, a widower who moved in with his young daughter, Christina.

Money was no object for Mason and he was able to do whatever he wanted with the house. He spent the first few years refurbishing the interior – without the help of a designer, instead choosing what he loved, mixing the best fixtures that money could buy. Mason's eclectic, opulent taste is evident as soon as you step into the grand entrance with its marble stairway. Other features include elaborate fireplaces, some with stunning over-mantles, carved mahogany doors, Lincrusta wallpapers, exquisite stained-glass windows, a decorative Moorish-style ceiling, parquet floors, marble staircases, floors and dado rails.

The tour introduces you to the building's fascinating history and Mason's family background. It also takes you into many of the rooms across the four-storey house, starting in the lavish entrance hall and finishing in the attic (once Mason's billiard room), which has an extended ceiling, stunning tiled fireplace, and sweeping views across the Hove rooftops out to sea.

Mr Mason lived at 33 Palmeira Mansions for 51 years until his death in 1940, outliving his second wife and marrying again in his 70s.

One of the paintings in Mason's collection, *Dante in Exile* by Lord Leighton, was bought for £1 million in 1990 at auction by Andrew Lloyd Webber, a record for a Leighton painting at that time.

A similar Moorish-style ceiling decorates the downstairs common room at the Foreign and Commonwealth Office in London.

BODHISATTVA KADAMPA MEDITATION CENTRE

A Buddhist village in Hove

3 Lansdowne Road, Hove BN3 1DN
Tel: 01273 732917
www.meditateinbrighton.com
Centre open daily from 11am. Peace Garden open most days from 9am to dusk

On first glance, passers-by might not know that this stunning Victorian mansion, tucked behind flint walls and surrounded by tall trees and a lush garden, is home to a thriving Buddhist community. It has a café, a bookshop, several meditation rooms, two shrine rooms and the largest statue of Buddha in East Sussex.

Walk up the long gravel drive and enter the lush gardens, however, and you find yourself in a peaceful haven, the bustle of the Western Road shops firmly behind you.

Built in the 19th century as a family house called Wick Lodge, the Bodhisattva headquarters has had many uses since then, including a boys' prep school, a girls' school, a convent, even the largest squat in England for a time, before Geshe Kelsang Gyatso established the Bodhisattva Kadampa Meditation Centre in 1992.

Everybody is welcome at the centre, which is open to the public every day, and offers a variety of Buddhist meditation classes, day courses, and weekend meditation retreats suitable for beginners and more experienced meditators. You don't have to commit to a course; you can just pop in and use its rooms for personal meditation, or browse the bookshop.

Its most charming feature is its 2-acre (0.8-hectare) award-winning Peace Garden, which is open to everyone most days from 9am until dusk. A wander through this tranquil space reveals lots of little flower-filled nooks, a fountain, a rose pergola, a circle of plum trees, a maritime garden, a pond, a lawn filled with picnic benches, and secluded areas with seats for quiet reflection.

Peace by the beach

The centre occasionally holds mini-meditation retreats at the Yellowave Clubhouse at 299 Madeira Drive, as well as free guided meditation sessions under the beautiful Grade II-listed bandstand in Hove as part of the Brighton Fringe Festival in May. Check the centre's website for details.

For a pleasant afternoon, take part in the lunchtime "Thought for the Day" meditation sessions, which are a bargain at £4. You can follow this with an excellent vegetarian lunch at the World Peace Café (open Tuesday to Friday 11am–4pm, and the occasional Saturday) before a wander through the garden.

WINSTON CHURCHILL PLAQUE

A reminder of Brighton's most famous resident

29–30 Brunswick Road, Hove BN1 1NR (on the corner of Lansdowne Road)

Winston Spencer Churchill is one of the most famous people in British history. What is less well known is that he went to school in Hove. This period in Brighton and Hove's history is marked by a blue plaque on the side of a building on the junction of Lansdowne Road and Brunswick Road.

According to Churchill's autobiography, *My Early Life*, his family decided to send him to preparatory school in the seaside town on the recommendation of Robson Roose, the family doctor. Roose practised in the town and suggested that "fresh sea air" would be good for the "delicate young Winston".

From 1883 to 1885, the future Prime Minister was educated at The Misses Thompson's Preparatory School. Run by two sisters, Kate and Charlotte Thompson, the school was located at 29–30 Brunswick Road, on the corner of Lansdowne Road.

In his autobiography, Churchill recalls fond memories of his schooling in Hove, which he enjoyed compared with other schools he had attended previously. "I was allowed to learn things which interested me: French, history, and lots of poetry by heart, and above all riding and swimming."

During the time that Churchill spent in Hove, the area around the school would have looked entirely different from what it does today. "At this time, Lansdowne Road was the northern boundary of the Brunswick area," says Peter Groves on the website "My Brighton and Hove". "Churchill's school was virtually on the outskirts of town, with open land to the north. At that point, St Ann's Well Gardens, yet to be opened as a public park, was called the Wick or Chalybeate. This was a wooded area with a medicinal spring, owned by Sir Julian Goldsmid."

After his school days, Churchill is known to have revisited the city several times: during the Second World War; in October 1947 for the Conservative Party Conference held at Brighton Dome; in November 1947 to receive the local "Freedom of the Borough of Brighton" tribute; and in 1952 to attend the Brighton Races.

Winston Churchill died on 24 January 1965. However, his memory and name live on in Brighton as Churchill Square, the town's main shopping centre, which is named after him.

THE REGENCY TOWN HOUSE

A Regency time capsule

13 Brunswick Square, Hove BN3 1EH
Tel: 01273 206306
www.rth.org.uk
Tours run throughout the year from April to October.
Events are held here all year: check the website for listings

Brighton was once Europe's most popular seaside spa, attracting wealthy Victorians to its shores for a dose of healthy sea air and a potter along one of its piers. Today, with its tacky seafront and neglected architecture, it's hard to imagine the fashionable destination it once was unless we look at old pictures.

The town's prosperous legacy is reflected in the grand Regency terraces that stretch along the seafront. Nowadays, most of them have been converted into flats, their original features lost to history. But if we head to Brunswick Square in Hove, history, architecture and nostalgia lovers are in for a real treat.

This is where you'll find some of the city's most stunning examples of Regency homes designed by an ambitious architect, Charles Busby. But most importantly, it's the site of a unique hidden gem.

Head to No. 13 Brunswick Square, where you can enjoy a tour of a Grade I-listed Regency property known as The Regency Town House. This once grand single-family home is currently being restored to its original state and developed as a "heritage centre" that will celebrate the architecture and social history of Brighton and Hove between the 1780s and 1840s.

The Town House was founded in the 1980s by conservationist, Nick Tyson, as a passion project. So far, the building has been reconverted from flats back to a single-family house and the restoration work, using traditional techniques, is in full swing.

"With the help of an army of dedicated volunteers and expertise, we're slowly and carefully returning this house to its former glory as funds become available. We raise these by running tours and hosting events," says Nick.

"The restoration is modelled on the traditional layout of the houses at the time," he adds. "These would have had servants' quarters in the basement, more formal rooms on the ground and first floors, and bedrooms on the floors above." There would also have been a coach house, a stable block and quarters for the coachmen and grooms at the back of the house.

"Layer upon layer of peeling paint has been removed, the plasterwork and mouldings repaired, and the original finishes analysed so we can use this knowledge to recreate the building and eventually offer full access to the house as it once stood." It is said he unlocked the gate with a gold key, claimed to be a replica of one of the original keys to the Royal Pavilion.

The Regency Dining Club (see p. 295) hosts various events based around Regency food, including "Dine Like a Servant".

HEADLESS STATUE

A forgotten beheaded tribute

Waterloo Street Arch and Gardens, Waterloo Street, Hove BN3 1AQ

Brighton is full of statues, but none is more bizarre and less widely known than this one without a head or hands, which stands just outside the Waterloo Street Arch (see p. 126).

Although today it might be met with odd looks from passers-by, the statue was once the full body of a man, complete with a head and two hands, the right one of which held a sword.

It was built as a monument to a young man called Capt. Samuel Pechell, whose father was MP for Brighton for over 25 years and an important figure in the local community. Capt. Pechell was a member of the Second Brigade, Light Division, 77th Regiment and was killed on duty at the Siege of Sevastopol during the Crimean War.

His death had a significant impact not only on the men of his regiment but also on the people of Brighton, who went into a period of mourning. In response to the collective grief, a statue was commissioned and paid for by public subscription, as was common in those days. This is the statue you see today, made out of Portland stone by the sculptor Matthew Noble. It once stood over 4 metres high.

The statue originally went on display in the Royal Pavilion, but poor Capt. Pechell has had several homes around Brighton since then. In 1914 he was moved to the entrance hall of Brighton Museum, then to the far end of the permanent sculpture gallery, before making his way to Preston Park, where he was beheaded at some point, for reasons unknown. Around 1940, he was finally put into storage at the Ranger's Yard in Stanmer Park, where he languished for a while until the Waterloo Street Community Garden group expressed an interest in giving him a new home in 2015.

Their original plan was to place the statue in the garden, but lifting him over or through the arch proved impossible. They had no choice but to put him on display where we see him today.

WATERLOO STREET ARCH AND GARDEN

An overlooked gateway to Hove's past

Waterloo Street, Hove BN3 1AQ

Nestled among the back streets of Hove is a curious stone archway leading to a tranquil hidden garden along the pathway to The Old Market theatre venue. It might look incongruous today, but this arch once marked an elaborate entryway to a riding academy and stables.

The Old Market – as its name suggests – originally opened in 1828 as a covered marketplace called The Market House, part of architect Charles Busby's prestigious Brunswick Town development of 1826. It was soon apparent that the market wasn't going to be successful, so it was quickly turned into stables and a riding school called Roberts Riding Academy. However, it wasn't until it was taken over by a Mr Alfred Du Pont that it truly flourished, Du Pont going on to buy the stables in the 1880s for £2,800.

The academy's reputation quickly grew far and wide, earning national acclaim, which meant it had to expand to keep up with demand. To reflect its new status, and to impress clients on their arrival, Du Pont built the Waterloo Street Arch.

By the early 1900s, however, The Old Market's equestrian heyday had passed. In the 1980s, after various modifications and having being used as a smokehouse, warehouse and garage, the building was ramshackle, grimy and full of asbestos.

The arch was given Grade II-listed status in 1971. Local residents eventually secured the funds to restore it, along with the main building, to commemorate its 150th anniversary. The work was completed in 1986.

It was further renovated in 2010 and reopened as The Old Market Theatre and performance venue.

An award-winning community garden

After the arch was restored, a community garden was set up to brighten up the pathway through the arch to The Old Market. Run by the Waterloo Street Community Garden group (WSCG), the garden has blossomed, even earning a coveted City In Bloom prize. A quirky statue has been installed at the entrance (see p. 124).
For more information on the garden, visit:
http://rossgeorge9.wixsite.com/wscg

ST ANDREW'S CHURCH

Home to a celestial surprise

Waterloo Street, Hove BN3 1AQ
www.visitchurches.org.uk
Open daily. For access, visitors must ask for the key at The Southern Belle pub
(tel: 01273 734806) opposite. The church is also occasionally open to the public
as a music venue.

In the early 1820s, the Prince Regent made the old fishing towns of Brighton and Hove fashionable places to be seen in. During this time, the Grade 1-listed St Andrew's Church – now closed for worship and only open on occasion to the public as a music venue – was built to serve the wealthy residents of the new Brunswick Estate and became one of the area's most fashionable places of worship.

Set back from the seafront, the Italian Renaissance-style symmetry and grandeur of this 1827 church (designed by the famous architect Sir Charles Barry) perfectly match the neighbouring squares and terraces.

The inside is just as pretty, with light streaming in through skylights and stained-glass windows, albeit a little altered since the church was built. The baldacchinos over the altar were added in 1925 by an architect called Randoll Blacking, along with a font to fulfil the parish priest's desire that St Andrew's should become "a little bit of Italy in Waterloo Street".

One of its most beautiful features is perhaps the painted ceiling, which features the sun surrounded by a crescent moon, a comet, Saturn and stars. A series of 19th-century monuments provides an introduction to the great and the good who worshipped here in the church's heyday.

As well as being a fashionable church, St Andrew's was a popular final resting place for members of Hove society, in an underground crypt. The crypt was closed for burials in 1854, by which time only 55 people had been buried there. Although access isn't possible today, it's said to house five segmented barrel vaults containing several rows of iron shelves on which hundreds of coffins could be placed.

Charles Barry plaque

Outside the church is a blue plaque commemorating the genius Victorian architect, Sir Charles Barry. He is said to have learned his craft in Brighton on much-loved buildings including St Andrew's Church as well as the Royal Sussex County Hospital and "the Pepperpot" (see p. 140) before going on to rebuild London's Palace of Westminster in the mid-19th century and design the Houses of Parliament. It's alleged he's buried here in the crypt.

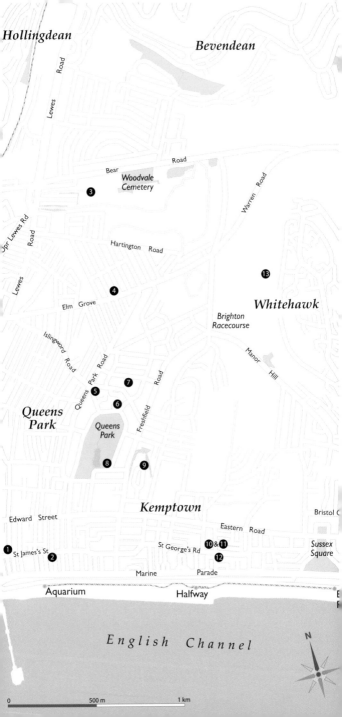

Kemptown to Whitehawk

① LITTLE FRIDGE LIBRARY   *132*

② AIDS MEMORIAL SCULPTURE   *134*

③ TOMB TRAIL   *136*

④ FEIBUSCH NATIVITY MURAL   *138*

⑤ THE PEPPERPOT   *140*

⑥ ATTREE VILLA TEMPLE   *142*

⑦ ST LUKE'S VICTORIAN SWIMMING BATHS   *144*

⑧ ROYAL SPA REMAINS   *146*

⑨ KEMP TOWN RAILWAY TUNNEL   *148*

⑩ FISHERMEN'S GALLERY   *150*

⑪ PEEL FAMILY CRYPT   *152*

⑫ SASSOON MAUSOLEUM   *154*

⑬ WHITEHAWK HILL   *156*

⑭ RACEHILL COMMUNITY ORCHARD   *158*

⑮ SECRET GARDEN KEMP TOWN   *160*

LITTLE FRIDGE LIBRARY

Brighton's smallest and most secret library

St James's Court, George Street, Brighton BN2 1RX
www.facebook.com/littlefridgelibrary%20
Open 24/7

Hidden up a little-known alleyway off the main high street in Kemptown is a small white fridge sitting beneath a cottage window. The words painted in black on the front read "Little Fridge Library". Open it up, and sure enough the shelves are stocked with books, which are free to take and pass on.

If the name sounds familiar, that's because it might remind you of the Little Free Library project that became popular a few years ago. Under this scheme, passers-by can take or leave books at the miniature libraries they find wherever they are in the world.

"I'd heard about the Little Free Library and thought it was a fantastic idea," says Laura Honeker, founder of the Little Fridge Library, "but I couldn't afford the subscription cost, so I decided to start my own" … which she did in early 2015. "I'm a total book magpie. I can't go past a bookshop or charity shop without going in. I read a lot and always have stacks of books that I need to donate to charity."

Laura also liked the idea that the project would help create a sense of community along the alleyway where she lives. "I threw a Dr Who themed party a few years ago and turned my front door into a Tardis, which drew people to see it. It unexpectedly created a sense of community spirit that I realised I missed. We don't see anyone walk past very often, so I thought the library would be good from this perspective too," she says.

"I was reading about anti-social architecture at the time and how isolating cities can be, especially for those with nowhere to go and no home, so it made even more sense to open it up. I sometimes put leaflets inside that give people in need information on public services they can draw on."

Anyone is free to peruse the library and take a book. "There's no need to sign up," says Laura. "You can just come along, have a browse and take what you want. I also really love the idea that people will share the books with everyone when they're finished."

Despite the fact that the library is outside her house, Laura rarely bumps into anyone taking a book. "People do leave me notes though, which is lovely," she says. "They're always positive, letting me know how much they like the idea for the library or loved the book they took. Some people have even left me poems, and I'll often go outside to discover another generous donation of books, so the library is always full of new stock."

AIDS MEMORIAL SCULPTURE

A lesser-known outdoor artwork

New Steine Gardens, Brighton BN2 1PA
www.romanymarkbruce.com

New Steine Gardens is a quiet leafy square offering respite from the busy streets of Kemptown, but it's also home to a touching and lesser-known landmark on the city's outdoor art map.

Tucked away at the St James's Street end of the gardens is a breathtaking 4-metre-high bronze statue called Tay. It depicts two intertwined figures, one male and one genderless, soaring elegantly up towards the sky to form a shadow in the shape of a red ribbon – the international symbol for HIV/AIDS awareness.

Commissioned by Brighton & Hove City Council as a memorial to those who have died of the disease, and to show support for those living with it, Tay was created by Romany Mark Bruce, a Brighton-based sculptor and painter. He was chosen by public ballot to create the piece, which was financed by private donations raised through community projects.

"I wanted to make something powerful and uplifting, rather than sombre," says Romany. His sculpture was unveiled on World AIDS Day in October 2009 by Elton John's civil partner David Furnish, a long-time supporter of HIV/AIDS charities through the Elton John AIDS Foundation.

According to Romany, "The support from the local community for this project has been incredible. Even though the piece is around 10 years old, people still get in touch to express their gratitude and praise for the memorial. In fact, only the other day I received a letter from a lady in Canada letting me know how beautiful she thinks the piece is, including a few pictures of her children playing near it. It's heart-warming to have been part of a project that gives people so much joy."

Making the piece wasn't without its challenges, though. "Before the sculpture was cast, I made a clay version which one day just completely collapsed on me. I lost half a tonne of clay and three months' work in a second," says Romany, "but I got on and rebuilt it, although, seven months later I nearly lost it again due to unusually freezing temperatures. I managed to save it this time. It took two years to finish in total."

For Romany, the best part about this project wasn't creating his first piece of public art, as he initially thought it would be. "Working on this memorial has given me the opportunity to commemorate my best friend, Paul Tay, whom I lost to AIDS when I was just 33 years old," he says. "I was always worried I'd forget him, but getting to make a public sculpture and name it after him has given me a way to remember."

TOMB TRAIL

A little-known nature walk through a haunting Victorian burial ground

Woodvale Cemetery, Lewes Road, Brighton BN2 3QB
Tel: 01273 604020
www.brighton-hove.gov.uk/content/community-and-life-events/
deaths-funerals-and-cemeteries/tomb-nature-trail
Open: April–Sept: Mon–Sat 9am–5.30pm, Sun 11am–5.30pm; Oct–March:
Mon–Sat 9am–4pm, Sun 11am–4pm

onsidering that the Woodvale Cemetery complex is set on 15 hectares in the middle of the city, it's unlikely you'll encounter other soul on a wander around … except perhaps the odd person sing it as a shortcut into town or leaving flowers on a loved-one's grave.

It's unusual to see people here simply taking in the magnificence this otherworldly early Victorian cemetery, let alone following the auntingly beautiful "tomb trail". You can find this in the leaflet *Lewes ad Cemeteries: A Walker's Guide* by local historian Maire McQueeney vailable from the Woodvale Cemetery office).

The trail is a circular walk that takes about an hour. It begins the left of the Extra-Mural Cemetery chapel and takes you up arrow steps and along winding steep paths lined with ivy-covered avestones, through a wildflower meadow and into the newer part of e cemetery. This is where burials still take place today and it offers onderful views across the whole site.

"When you're in our quiet, deserted grounds, it's easy to forget that u're in the middle of a busy city," says cemeteries officer William Mason.

Most of the cemetery is typically Victorian, built at the peak of the ty's economic power. It's filled with a wonderful variety of elaborate and corative Victorian crypts, tombs and graves. There are mausoleums mmissioned by the wealthy families of politicians, performers, istocrats and decorated soldiers – even a celebrated circus master.

"We have a number of notable local people buried here: you can ot their graves by using our walking guide," says William. "The graves clude that of a local brewing family called the Tamplins; councillor orothy Stringer; the Cox family, who owed Cox's Pill Factory, now the e of Lewes Road Sainsbury's; and Smith Hannington, founder of the d Hanningtons department store, to name just a few. Perhaps what's ost surprising, although not at all well known, is that the funeral of the ritish occultist, Aleister Crowley, took place here."

As well as its history of notable burials and bizarre funerals, Woodvale home to a plethora of wildlife. "We regularly see jays and woodpeckers re," says William, "and BBC Springwatch visited a couple of years ago study the badgers and foxes who make their home here."

EARBY

n unusual lunch spot

fter you've completed the trail, ponder the meaning of life over a sandwich the cemetery picnic garden overlooking the Extra-Mural Cemetery.

FEIBUSCH NATIVITY MURAL

A heavenly resurrection

St Wilfrid's Flats, Whippingham Road, Brighton BN2 3PZ
Can be viewed during Heritage Open Days weekends. For more information,
visit www.rth.org.uk
Admission free

n the former Lady Chapel of St Wilfrid's Church is a long-forgotten religious mural of the nativity, which was recently unearthed after 37 ears. It was painted in 1939 by Hans Feibusch, a prolific modernist German-Jewish artist who fled to England from the Nazis.

When builders began converting St Wilfrid's into social housing in 015, they discovered a heavenly sight: this huge mural measuring over 6 square metres and covering three walls of the original Lady Chapel on ne ground floor.

The artwork was in poor condition when it was found by the Hyde roup housing association, with extensive water damage to the paintwork nd plaster, caused partly by a leak in one of the walls. However, a successful rowd-funding campaign raised £28,000 to pay for the restoration work.

The restored mural was formally unveiled by author Alison MacLeod, hose novel *Unexploded* was inspired by Feibusch's life and is set around nis area in Brighton. It's based around a character called Otto, who is ommissioned by the real-life Bishop George Bell of Chichester to create mural for St Wilfrid's.

Feibusch was born in Frankfurt in 1898, and after his studies became n active member of several prominent artists' societies in Germany in the

920s and 1930s. In 1930 he was warded the German Grand State rize for Painters by the Prussian academy of Arts in Berlin, but with the rise to power of the Nazis, is work was outlawed.

When he arrived in Britain, eibusch designed posters and ook jackets for Shell and the London Underground. Bishop Bell spotted his work and wrote o ask if he would paint a mural or St Wilfrid's.

Feibusch went on to become videly known as a church muralist nd sculptor. He died in 1998 hortly before his 100th birthday.

St Wilfrid's Church itself is unique in that the style is said to show influences of the Scottish architects Richard Norman Shaw and Charles Rennie Mackintosh.

THE PEPPERPOT

A striking architectural oddity ...

Junction of Queen's Park Road and Tower Road
Can be viewed from the outside 24/7
Occasionally open to the public during Heritage Open Days weekends. For
more information, visit www.rth.org.uk organised by the Regency Town House
www.rth.org.uk/BHOD17

Currently standing damp, dark and empty at the north-west entrance of Queen's Park is an unusual structure that looks a bit like a pepper dispenser on a plinth, hence its nickname around town as the "Pepperpot".

Designed by Sir Charles Barry in around 1830, this unusual 10-sided, 8-metre-high Grade II-listed building has Corinthian pillars and a cupola. According to the Friends of the Pepperpot, it was built as a water or observation tower for Attree Villa, the former home of the wealthy Brighton businessman and landowner, Sir Thomas Attree.

An encyclopedia from 1830 with the snappy title *Arcana of Science, Or, An Annual Register of Useful Inventions and Improvements, Discoveries And New Facts, In Mechanics, Chemistry, Natural History and Social Economy* describes it as a "beautiful edifice called Belvedere Tower" and suggests it was "built for the purpose of enclosing a steam engine …". It's thought that this engine would have been used to draw water from a well below.

Vague historical records show that the structure has had other uses since then. From 1863, a Brighton man named George Duddell – who once owned the nearby Attree Villa (see p. 142) – is alleged to have used it to house the Brighton Mail printing and publishing house. Others suggest it was used as a military observation post during the Second World War, scout headquarters and later an artist's studio.

In 1952 Brighton & Hove City Council carried out extensive repairs and was considering opening the building to the public, although this hasn't happened. In the 1960s, the single-storey extension opposite its entrance was converted into a public toilet, although it's not in use today.

A map of the area dating back to 1863 shows that the Pepperpot was once surrounded by a wall. A large tank was buried on its west side to store the water drawn from the well, and a tunnel connected it with Attree Villa.

The Friends of the Pepperpot

This community group was established in 2010 by a team of volunteers concerned with the condition of the Pepperpot. Their aim is to continue lobbying Brighton & Hove City Council to preserve the building's heritage. To find out more, visit their Facebook page, here:
www.facebook.com/Friends-of-the-Pepperpot-327975608727/

ATTREE VILLA TEMPLE

Elegant remains of an Italian-style estate

Carn Court, North Drive, Brighton BN2 0HR

Opposite the north entrance to Queen's Park, inside the car park of an ordinary block of modern flats, is one of the few remaining relics of Brighton's finest mansion.

This Italianate rectangular structure, with its domed roof and Ionic pillars, is often referred to as the Attree Villa temple. Incongruous in today's surroundings, it once stood in the garden of the Attree Villa, a large estate belonging to Sir Thomas Attree, a wealthy and prestigious Brighton lawyer who counted the royal family and the Pavilion Estate among his clients. In fact, he was so wealthy that he bought what was then Brighton Park, renaming it Queen's Park before commissioning the renowned architect Sir Charles Barry – best known for designing the Houses of Parliament – to design his estate at the park, which included the Attree Villa temple.

The villa was built in 1830 and would have been an elegant sight, with its shallow roof, broad eaves, plain walls, loggia with three round-headed glass doors and a balustraded terrace. Sir Thomas died here in 1863, aged 85. Although in the same year another local businessman called George Duddell is said to have bought it, it remained empty for around 20 years until it reopened in 1909 as a Xaverian College for Catholic boys.

The college closed in 1966 and the villa was left to decay, before being demolished in 1972 despite its Grade II-listed status. Sadly, only a few relics remain, including some old walls and gateposts in Queen's Park Terrace and Attree Drive, the two entrances to the park, and this temple building, which is said to have originally contained the statue of a seated dog.

Brighton's longest-running business

Thomas Attree and his younger brother worked for their father William's law firm, Attree and Son, at 8 Ship Street. Now practising under the name of Howlett Clarke, it's the oldest business in Brighton. Another Attree brother, Harry, founded the *Brighton Herald* in 1806. It was the first newspaper in the country to announce the British victory at the Battle of Trafalgar.

ST LUKE'S VICTORIAN SWIMMING BATHS

The only Victorian baths left in Brighton …

St Luke's Terrace, Brighton BN2 9ZE
Tel: 01273 602385
www.freedom-leisure.co.uk/centres/st-lukes-swimming-pool/
Open daily

Public swimming baths saw a huge boom in the late Victorian era. Although Brighton has several public pools, St Luke's Swimming Baths is the only one in the city remaining from this era, and also one of only 14 Victorian pools left in the country.

Set in a typical red-brick building of the time, and surrounded by a fine set of original Victorian wrought-iron railings, the pool forms part of an impressive complex that includes St Luke's primary school – once a boarding school – and a former caretaker's house. Built between 1900 and 1903, the buildings were designed by Thomas Simpson, the Brighton and Preston School Board's architect at the time.

Today, the pool is popular with adults and is still well used by the

St Luke's schoolchildren, even though it's administratively detached from the school and run by Freedom Leisure on behalf of Brighton & Hove City Council.

Two adjoining former classrooms have been incorporated to provide changing rooms – individual cubicles would have originally lined the perimeter of the pool hall. Inside, although the pool itself has been modernised, the original wooden Victorian balcony still survives, if somewhat truncated. The metal roof is concealed above a suspended ceiling, but there's still no mistaking the fact you're swimming in a historic building.

The 1000-year swim

In summer 2008, Victorian Society Director Dr Ian Dungavell successfully completed an epic challenge to highlight the importance of public swimming pools. He visited each listed Victorian and Edwardian pool still open to the public in England and swam a lap in each one for every year that the building had been standing.

His challenge started on Thursday 24 July with 104 laps at Bramley Baths in Leeds. He finished by swimming 116 laps at Dulwich Leisure Centre in south-east London. Throughout summer 2008, Dungavell swam 1,543 laps at 14 pools, covering a distance more than the equivalent of crossing the Dover Strait in the English Channel.

ROYAL SPA REMAINS

A reminder of Brighton's spa-town history

Queens Park, Brighton, BN2

When German doctor and chemist Frederick Struve almost accidentally poisoned himself with cyanide in his laboratory in the early 1800s, he set out on a desperate tour of all the European health spas to regain his health.

Once recovered, his positive experience inspired him to use his knowledge of medicine and chemistry to recreate European spa waters, which he carbonated in his factory. He then set out to make his fortune curing the sick and ailing folk of Eastern Europe by opening spas in Moscow, Berlin and St Petersburg and then … Brighton.

Remains of the detox spa he opened here in 1824 – called the Royal Spa – can be found in Queens Park, in the form of a Romanesque temple, whitewashed, with six columns on the front and five arched openings.

Around this time, Brighton was a fashionable seaside town, well known around the world as a place to come and benefit from its curative properties. The new wealthy visitors flocked to this detox temple, which they would enter through double glass doors in the first arch to find – according to Brighton Town Press's curious book *The Story of Queen's Park, Brighton* – a "handsome room of some 50 or 60 feet in length, with a high ceiling, plaster mouldings and chandeliers. The colours were lilac, grey and opal with the plaster decoration picked out in gold."

Historical pictures of the interior show a polished oak floor and 15 brass taps that served the various waters behind a long mahogany bar, each one believed to cure specific illnesses.

It's also suggested that visiting the temple was as much a social event as a medical one. As the photographs and paintings show, up to 100 horse-drawn carriages could be seen at any one time, parked up on Spa Hill (now Park Street).

In 1978, following a vigorous campaign by the Queens Park community, the shell of the building was saved. It now stands in the grounds of the Royal Spa Nursery School, designed and built by local architect Tim Williams. He hoped that the colonnade could be used for community events, such as open-air theatre performances.

KEMP TOWN RAILWAY TUNNEL

The entrance to an abandoned railway line

*Storage Box Brighton, Freshfield Industrial Estate, Freshfield Road, Brighton
BN2 0LE*
*Open: To visit, contact Storage Box Brighton. Alternatively, tours take place
during the Heritage Open Days weekends. For more information, email Kevin
Wilsher: kevin@rth.org.uk*
Admission free

Although there's an obvious clue in the form of a large bronze train protruding from the nearby Gala Bingo Hall, most people passing through this part of town are unaware that this was once the site of the old Kemp Town railway station.

Evidence of this can be found in a hidden corner of the Freshfield Industrial Estate: here you can still see the old Kemp Town railway tunnel entrance, through which a short branch line serving the Kemptown District ran from 1869 to 1932.

The London to Brighton line opened in 1841 and proved so successful, that other railway companies (such as the London, Chatham and Dover Railway) started to show an interest in running their own lines into Brighton. To strengthen its position and fend off competition, the London, Brighton and South Coast Railway (which already ran the London to Brighton line) successfully proposed building a branch line to serve Kemptown.

The branch line started at London Road station, travelled through a tunnel at Ditchling Road, across a 14-arch viaduct over Lewes Road and a three-arch viaduct over Hartington Road, before entering the 900-metre-long Kemp Town tunnel (which runs underneath Elm Grove through the cliffs), emerging in the corner of what's now Freshfield Industrial Estate. The Kemp Town railway station would have been located where the Gala Bingo car park is today.

The line cost £100K to build – about £50 million in today's terms – had a single track, and ran about five passenger trains a day, costing 6 old pence for a first-class ticket and 2 old pence for third class.

It operated between 1869 and 1932, closing on the same day that the steam trains stopped running on the London to Brighton line. This allowed them to close quietly, although the line stayed open for freight until 1971.

After it closed permanently, the track was lifted, the line bought by the Brighton Corporation and the station building demolished.

Today, the tunnel is a storage facility, but it has also been used as an air-raid shelter during the Second World War and as a mushroom farm.

FISHERMEN'S GALLERY

The best secret seats in the house ...

St George's Church, St George's Road, Brighton BN2 1ED
www.stgeorgesbrighton.com
Open daily, times vary: check with the church

St George's Church is unusual in that although it's a popular Anglican church, it's also a well-known quirky performance and live music venue, used regularly to host concerts and other events since 2001.

The church is one of the main venues for bands that come to play around Brighton for the Great Escape Festival, which takes place at various venues around the city in April each year. It's also a popular choice for other gatherings, like giant sewing circles.

Some of the best concert seats in the house are up in the incredible fishermen's gallery, which can be found high above the entrance to the church. Hidden behind the main balcony, it's accessible via two internal curved staircases, one each side of the central vestibule with cast-iron balustrades.

This curiously named feature was added in the 1830s by Queen Adelaide, consort to William IV, the last British King of Hanover. She used the church as her Chapel Royal on Sunday afternoons and needed to accommodate the growing congregation. As the name implies, fishermen were made to sit up in the gallery due to its remote location, to stop their stench filling the church.

"Brighton was very much a fishing town when the church was built, and the fishermen would come straight off the boats and into church, so you can imagine the state of them," says Marcia Carey, treasurer of St George's. "Queen Adelaide would sit up in the balcony and is said to have arranged for the fishermen's gallery to be built behind her so that they could sit and enjoy the service without their odour disrupting her enjoyment – or so the story goes."

NEARBY
The lampposts of St George's

Outside St George's western entrance is a Grade II-listed matching pair of electricity-powered cast-iron lampposts dating back to the early or mid-19th century. Once powered by gas, these types of lampposts were common outside buildings in the early Victorian era (see p. 18).

PEEL FAMILY CRYPT

A burial vault in a community centre

*Kemp Town Crypt Community Centre, St George's Church,
93 St George's Road, Brighton BN2 1ED
Tel: 01273 279448
www.stgeorgesbrighton.com
Viewable by appointment: contact the church for more information
Admission free*

Back in the late 1800s, Thomas Read Kemp, the founder of Kemp Town, sold his stake in St George's Church to an illustrious Brighton resident called Lawrence Peel. Lawrence was the son of former Prime Minister and founder of the Metropolitan Police, Sir Robert Peel, who lived in Sussex Square (see p. 160).

When Lawrence Peel died in 1888, the church passed to his son, Charles Lennox Peel. The following year, he sold it to the congregation for £4,000, reserving the underground vault as the final resting place for the Peel family.

However, it wasn't until as recently as the late 1990s that this curious crypt was rediscovered. "The story goes that it was found by accident when the new community centre building was added some time in the late 1990s," says Marcia Carey, treasurer of St George's.

"Apparently the builders were digging and stumbled on it. The gate is thought to be original, although when the builders found it, it was covered over. It's hard to find out any more information about it as a fire at the Peel family home meant most of their photos and documents were destroyed."

Today, thanks to a Heritage Lottery Fund grant, the Peel family crypt has been completely renovated and restored for people to visit. Strangely, this busy, modern community centre underneath one of Kemptown's most attractive and popular churches has become the setting for this unusual, little-known sight.

You'll find it at the end of a corridor behind a green iron gate, which remains locked, but you can get a good look at what's inside through the iron bars. There's a gold statue of an eagle, a few pieces of furniture and several memorial tablets to the various members of the Peel family on the north wall and the east end, with space remaining for a few more.

Kemp Town or Kemptown?

The use of these two different place name spellings throughout is intentional. Kemp Town refers to Thomas Kemp's original 19th-century Kemp Town Estate, today known as the Kemp Town Conservation Area. Kemptown refers to the wider modern district.

The community centre walls are also a gallery for a quirky display called "Kemptown through the Looking Glass", which includes snippets and anecdotes from locals. According to one story, flowers and cards from Lawrence Peel's funeral were found in the chapel some time in the 1990s – a few are on display in cases around the main chapel building.

SASSOON MAUSOLEUM

A family tomb turned cabaret venue

83 St George's Road, Brighton BN2 1EF
www.proudcabaret.com

Next time you're out enjoying a spot of dinner and entertainment courtesy of Proud Cabaret, stop to reflect on the setting – for you're actually in a Grade II-listed former grave, better known as the Sassoon mausoleum, a fancy oriental-style structure complete with a pagoda roof topped with a vase and finial.

Sir Albert Sassoon was a member of the prominent Anglo-Indian Jewish family of entrepreneurs who founded the Sassoon & Co banking firm, as well as various well-known silk and cotton factories, the Port Canning Company and the first dock to be built in western India – Sassoon Dock – in former Bombay.

As well as a plush home in Kensington, London, close to the office of the family business, from 1876 Albert also had a home at 1 Eastern Terrace in Kemptown at the junction of St George's Road and Paston Place.

Thinking ahead, he arranged for a mausoleum to be built in the garden: this is the fancy oriental-style structure resembling the Royal Pavilion we see today, where he was buried in 1896, followed by his son, Sir Edward, who was laid to rest next to him in 1912.

In 1933 Albert's body was moved to a Jewish cemetery in London when his grandson, Sir Philip Sassoon, sold the house and garden. The building has had various uses since then, including an air-raid shelter during the Second World War and a decorator's store. In 1949 it was bought by the Kemp Town Brewery and turned into the Bombay Bar, the sign for which you can still see over the door on Paston Place. In the 1970s it became a nightclub.

Between 1999 and 2000, the building was restored with the help of a Historic England grant, reopening in 2001 as a music venue called the Hanbury Ballroom. This closed in 2010 and reopened the following year as Proud Cabaret.

Sir Albert Sassoon was made a Companion of the Order of the Star of India in 1867 – a star motif can be seen in the Sassoon windows that decorate the Middle Street Synagogue, to which Sir Albert was a donor (see p. 68).

Proud Cabaret is known for hosting its events in unusual venues. These include the south gallery of a 200-year-old horse hospital in Camden's Stables Market in north London.

WHITEHAWK HILL

A lush inner-city escape hiding a remarkable ancient sight

Off Manor Hill, Brighton BN2 5EH

Whitehawk Hill occupies a commanding spot just south of Brighton Racecourse, with sweeping views over Brighton and Hove. This lush hidden gem is one of the city's richest wildlife sites, filled with beautiful wildflower meadows that attract large numbers of butterflies. It's home to the hugely successful Racehill Community Orchard (see p. 158) – and a resident flock of grazing sheep, which like to huddle on the main hill or the Tenantry Down triangle.

It's also the setting for an unusual ancient sight – the home of Brighton's very first inhabitants and Britain's earliest Stone Age settlement. Archaeologists believe that Whitehawk Camp, as it's known today, was chosen some 5,500 years ago as the site for a series of curious circular ditches and banks – said to be evidence of an ancient culture and one of Britain's first farming communities.

Although only a small part of Whitehawk Camp has been excavated, the findings show evidence of seasonal gatherings, the marking of territorial ownership and the consumption of meat. The site was apparently important enough to become the final resting place for members of the local tribes.

Most findings were unearthed on digs carried out in the late 1920s and early 30s. They include the remains of four complete burials, the bodies of an 8-year-old child and a young woman alongside the remains of her newborn child, huge numbers of Stone Age flint tools, pieces of pottery, the bones of oxen, cattle, pigs and deer, and other fragmentary human remains.

In 2014, a 12-month Heritage Lottery-funded project was launched to bring the findings up to date. In addition to a fresh site dig, the scheme involved photographing the objects excavated during the 1920s and 30s and packing them for storage. Some of the items catalogued are accessible on the Brighton Museums' digital media bank portal by typing "Whitehawk" into the search box.

Archaeological history tours of the Whitehawk Camp site take place as part of the Heritage Open Days weekends – all free to explore. Events in Brighton are organised by the Regency Town House (see p. 122). Programme details are posted on its website around three months in advance: www.rth.org.uk/BHOD17

RACEHILL COMMUNITY ORCHARD

A fruity hidden gem …

Whitehawk Nature Reserve, Swanborough Drive, Brighton BN2 5QB
https://brightonpermaculture.org.uk/orchards/racehill/aboutracehill
Open daily from dawn to dusk
Admission free

Hidden from plain sight almost in the middle of the Whitehawk Estate is one of the city's best-kept urban secrets. It nestles on 3 acres (1.2 hectares) of lush, wild landscape overlooking the city and the sea known as the Whitehawk Nature Reserve. The Racehill Community Orchard is a collection of 200 fruit trees – once established, they could reap an estimated 3–4 tonnes of fruit a year.

The scheme was launched in January 2013 after 80 per cent of people who replied to a public consultation (conducted by Brighton & Hove Food Partnership's Harvest Project) said they would like to see an orchard here.

It was originally managed by a community group of local people who volunteered regularly to plant trees and undertake conservation activities, but it's now run by the Brighton Permaculture Trust.

"We've planted many varieties of trees," says project manager, Stephan Gehrels, "… apples, pears, plums, maybe a few cherries and some of the more unusual trees, like figs."

It's a marvellous place to discover, have a wander around and take in the view across Brighton – or even get involved with. "There are always lots of jobs to do, from planting the trees in wintertime through to summer, when we maintain them. This involves weeding around young trees, watering them, and managing vegetation, including scything," says Stephan.

"This mainly involves being around nice people, chatting, enjoying hard work, and then relaxing after the hard work. It's a pleasant environment and a way of escaping town life. Mainly it's a nice feeling to know the work we're doing will help the community."

As well as a great source of fruit, the combination of fruit trees, grassland, scrub and other features of the orchard makes it an excellent wildlife habitat. An abundance of animals and insects have been spotted within several hundred metres of the Racehill site, including slow worms, adders and small birds known as dunnocks.

Volunteering at Racehill Community Orchard

The Orchard holds regular volunteer days, with activities varying each week depending on the season. These include mulching or watering trees, spotting interesting bits of wildlife, flowers and edible plants, clearing scrub, scything and picking up litter. To get involved, visit the Brighton Permaculture website – details above on the opposite page.

SECRET GARDEN KEMP TOWN

The city's only outdoor sculpture park

Corner of Bristol Gardens and Bristol Place, Brighton BN2 5JE
www.secretgardenkemptown.co.uk
Open for pre-arranged exhibitions and events: see website for details

Most of the grand buildings on Kemp Town's stunning Sussex Square are now flats, but there was a time when they were single-family homes. Some of them shared extensive gardens that would have been linked by a tunnel to the owner's property.

What is now known as the Secret Garden Kemp Town was once part of a garden around three times the size belonging to 32 Sussex Square. This large townhouse was owned by Lawrence Peel, younger brother of Robert (founder of the Metropolitan Police force). Around 1830, he commissioned a "pleasure garden", complete with tennis courts and a kitchen garden.

In 1950, concerned for the garden's future, Regency Society founder Dr Antony Dale bought it and cared for it along with his wife, Yvonne. It was her wish that the garden would never be sold for development, but would always remain a haven for the community in the form of an arts venue. Together with Regency Society chairman Gavin Henderson (former artistic director of Brighton Festival), they came up with the idea of creating a sculpture park run by a board of trustees, which would secure funding to realise their plan and continue their work.

Today, their vision has been realised. The Secret Garden Kemp Town is now a unique community arts venue, the only garden of its type in the city – where major outdoor works of sculpture are shown in a secure setting. It comes alive every year for the Brighton Festival and opens regularly for temporary art exhibitions featuring work by emerging artists.

What was once mainly lawn has been completely redesigned by the venue's resident gardener, Nick Dwyer. The area features beds filled with plenty of seasonal colour and traditional perennials mixed with contemporary architectural plants, as well as apple, mulberry, quince and medlar trees. There's also a lovely covered area built against the garden's west flint wall (used to host gatherings) and a bench from the West Pier standing on the lawn.

Sound sculptures by Hamish Black were the first works to go on display. They included a 10m-long artwork called *Black Blackbird*, modelled on the sound a blackbird makes and built out of 200 semicircular discs cut from the remains of an elm tree blown down in Brighton during the 1987 storm. Another installation, entitled Kick, represents the sound of a kick recorded in stereo.

North Laine to Round Hill

1. THE GHOST OF JENNY LIND SCULPTURE   *164*
2. RICHARDSON'S YARD   *166*
3. BRIGHTON GREENWAY   *168*
4. ANTIQUE SAFE AT THE DUKE'S   *170*
5. CAMDEN TERRACE   *172*
6. BRIGHTON TOY AND MODEL MUSEUM   *174*
7. SUSSEX MASONIC CENTRE   *176*
8. LOAVES AND FISHES SCULPTURE   *178*
9. JEW STREET   *180*
10. THE OLD VICARAGE   *182*
11. FORMER ISETTA FACTORY SITE   *184*
12. SILVER ALTAR   *186*
13. THE GARDEN HOUSE   *188*
14. MAX MILLER ROOM   *190*
15. IRELAND'S GARDENS GATEWAY   *192*
16. ROUND HILL CATS' CREEP   *193*
17. SHOE TREE   *194*
BENJAMIN JAMES SMITH HOUSE
(SEE ENTRY FOR LOCATION DETAILS)   *196*

THE GHOST OF JENNY LIND SCULPTURE

An unexpected ghostly appearance …

Brighton Greenway, New England Road, Brighton BN1

Set on an abandoned Victorian cast-iron railway bridge over New England Road is an eerie vision of a ghost train. This two-dimensional sculpture is a replica of the Jenny Lind locomotive, one of the very first 10 steam engines built in 1847 by locomotive-manufacturing company E.B. Wilson for the new London, Brighton and South Coast Railway, and named after the famous Swedish opera singer.

The piece was created by Brighton artist Jon Mills as part of the New England Quarter redevelopment. It was designed to celebrate Brighton's railway history, and as a reminder of the old locomotive works site once located here. Mills used black-and-white Victorian etchings as the inspiration for his ghost train sculpture, coating its steel body in four different shades of grey to create a similar eerie etched effect. To add to the ghostlike appeal, uplighters installed around it come on at night and slowly fade up and down to make the train look as though it's appearing and disappearing. Mills made the wheels and undercarriage before adding the details, like the fretwork mudguard, firebox, drive linkages and leaf spring on the front. It only took a year to complete, but wasn't installed until eight years later – for 30 months, it had been sitting complete in Mills' yard, waiting for Network Rail to agree installation access.

The original *Jenny Lind* locomotive design proved so successful that train-manufacturing company E.B. Wilson adopted it as its standard design. More than 70 of these locomotives were built for various railways, including 24 for the Midland Railway.

The abandoned railway bridge on which the *Jenny Lind* sculpture is displayed forms part of the Brighton Greenway, a green corridor and pedestrian walkway running between Brighton station and New England Road. The bridge itself was built in 1852 and is one of the earliest surviving railway bridges with cast-iron arches. See p. 168 for more information.

Jon Mills' metalworks can be found all over the UK. Fabricated in steel, they range from stand-alone high-street sculptures and sculptural railings on civic buildings to 1-inch-high props for children's books. Hundreds of his mileposts stand on the Sustrans National Cycle Network. In recent years, Mills has received several commissions in his home town of Brighton, including works for the Millennium Brighton Festival, St Bartholomew's school and Hove Museum.

RICHARDSON'S YARD

Container town

New England Road, Brighton BN1 4GG

The site of the former Cobbler's Thumb pub has become the location for an unusual hub known as Richardson's Yard – named after the neighbouring scrap-metal merchant.

It consists of two stacks of recycled shipping containers – their brightly coloured corrugated walls and porthole windows conceal low-cost homes for a community of former homeless people. Along with its stony beach and gigantic seagulls, Brighton's other defining factor is its huge homeless population, which this scheme was designed to ease.

Completed in December 2013, Richardson's Yard was developed by property company QED Estates for Brighton Housing Trust to provide "moving-on" accommodation for Brighton's homeless in the form of 36 shipping containers, stacked into a five-storey mobile housing estate. A year later, nine more containers were added; they are currently used for office and community space.

The containers are commonly used as homes in Amsterdam, as student flats, accommodation for the Salvation Army – and even as a hotel. The Brighton containers were originally converted for a social housing project in Holland in 2010, but the order to Tempohousing was cancelled due to funding problems.

Green roofs

Next time you're strolling along Brighton Greenway (see p. 168), when you approach the start of the disused railway bridge, stop and look down onto the Richardson's Yard containers and you'll notice their green roofs. These wildflower "roof gardens" are planted up to change with the seasons and provide insulation for people staying on the top floor of the development. In addition to fruit trees, the site has several raised planting beds and areas in which to grow food. This scheme is supported by the Brighton Housing Trust's Grow! initiative, which also runs on-site gardening sessions.

BRIGHTON GREENWAY

An intriguing inner-city escape

Between Brighton station and New England Road
www.brightongreenway.uk
Admission free

Until 2014, the area between Brighton railway station and New England Road was a deserted wasteland. Today, it has been transformed into a lush miniature pedestrian and cycle route called Brighton Greenway, offering the setting for a pleasant urban stroll with access to London Road and Preston Circus.

The greenway follows the route of a Victorian railway track that once ran through Brighton's celebrated locomotive works, which flourished between 1852 and 1958 and employed 2,500 people.

When the works closed, the site was occupied by Isetta (see p. 184) until 1964 and eventually demolished five years later. The area was left derelict until 2004, but designated a protected wildlife area in 1995. When the New England Quarter was developed, Brighton & Hove City Council negotiated with landowners Sainsbury's and Network Rail to allow public access along the walkway.

Today, it's a worthwhile amble along the section leading to Brighton station. The meadow-style planting features sustainable ornamental plants, such as smoke bush, yarrow and red bistort, designed to attract local wildlife. Stone-filled gabion baskets offer a habitat for insects and native reptiles.

The eastern side of the greenway is also designed to attract wildlife. It features mature trees (retained when the site was developed) alongside new shrubs, including holly, hawthorn bushes and ivy planted to grow over the Victorian pathways.

Wildflowers suited to chalk grasslands – including cowslip, red valerian and wild carrot – have been sown or allowed to grow naturally. They support a wide diversity of insects and birds and look lovely in the spring when they bloom.

Features of the greenway

Scattered throughout Brighton Greenway are several public artworks and landscaping features, including Jon Mills' mysterious *Ghost Train* (also known as *The Ghost of Jenny Lind*) set on a disused railway bridge over New England Road (see p. 164). You'll also notice the concrete fossil-shaped seats designed by Rachel Reynolds, with help from children at the nearby St Bartholomew's primary school, some geometric stone sculptures that double up as seating, and a length of railings based on a rack of clinker shovels (pictured).

ANTIQUE SAFE AT THE DUKE'S

A mysterious relic in the UK's oldest cinema

Duke of York's Picturehouse, Preston Road, Brighton BN1 4NA
www.picturehouses.com/cinema/Duke_Of_Yorks

If there's one building that stands out among the architectural mish-mash around Preston Circus, it's the Duke of York's Picturehouse, not only for the giant *Can Can* legs on its roof, but also for its ornate Edwardian baroque-style façade.

The Duke's, as it's known locally, opened in 1910 and is acknowledged to be the oldest surviving purpose-built cinema in the UK, having operated for over 100 years without a break.

It's a favourite with the city's fans of independent cinema, although most don't notice a beautiful old Victorian safe on the lobby floor between the two entrances, piled with flyers and leaflets. A little research reveals that this Milners Patent Fire Resistant Safe might date back to 1910 – around the time the cinema opened. Its provenance is a mystery, though, so it's nice to imagine that this mysterious relic once belonged to the cinema's founder, a lady called Violet Melnotte Wyatt, a well-known stage performer of the early 1900s. Together with her Gilbert and Sullivan performer husband, Frank Wyatt, they owned the Duke of York's Theatre in London. There was no cinema in Brighton at the time and Violet, convinced that there was a fortune to be made, is well known for exclaiming: "I want an electric theatre!"

In 1908, Violet and Frank commissioned Clayton & Black to design the cinema on the site of the old Longhurst Brewery at Preston Circus – for £3,000. After two years the new cinema opened on 22 September 1910 to a crowd of 2,000 people. The first screening was a hybrid film combining a magic lantern show, narration and a short film programme of dramas, comedies and topical Pathé newsreels, accompanied by music from a celesta organ.

Today, the cinema seats 278 people, but in its heyday it seated over 800 and looked very different. According to historian Allen Eyles in the book, *The Duke's at 100: The Story of Brighton's Favourite Cinema*, "… there was once a ticket booth between the doors, where customers would buy tickets before going inside. The foyer was small and there were two shops to each side; one selling French pastries delivered daily by the ferry from Dieppe to Brighton's West Pier; the other selling cigarettes, cigars and confectionery." Ayles also notes Stan the cinema's page boy as saying, "The Dukes was really beautiful. There were goldfish swimming in the tanks in the foyer and ferns and plants, and everything used to be highly polished".

Unfortunately, the Wyatts were insolvent by 1911 so had to sell the cinema to a wealthier owner, but the Duke of York's Cinema would never have existed if it wasn't for Violet's vision.

CAMDEN TERRACE

Brighton's most beautiful secret alleyway

Brighton BN1

Brighton is filled with little secret alleyways sandwiched between other streets and known locally as "twittens". Some are well known, others less so. The most beautiful – and surprisingly, one of the least trodden – is Camden Terrace in West Hill close to Brighton station.

With its rows of Mediterranean-style whitewashed cottages built in the 1840s, other larger homes and lush greenery, a stroll along it transports you to a different world. It also makes a great alternative route to the tourist-laden Queen's Road that runs to and from the station.

A nice way to discover the city's hidden corners is to navigate your way around via this collection of secret passageways. Besides Camden Terrace, there are others that are less known and are worth hunting out, such as Vine Place and Lewis's Buildings. Some are embarrassingly dingy and dank, while everyone has their favourite. The best known are arguably Black Lion Lane, Ship Street Gardens, Boundary Passage off Western Road – while you're there, look for the boundary stone at the Lansdowne Road end (see p. 14) – Gloucester Passage, Crown Gardens and Zion Gardens.

The meaning of the word "twitten" is widely known – *The Dictionary of Sussex Dialect* from 1875 describes it as "a narrow path between two walls or hedges" – yet its origins are unclear. Reports suggest it derives either from the Anglo-Saxon "twicen", meaning a place where two roads meet, or from "twitchel", a word used in the north Midlands in the 14th century to mean a forked road. It's also often said to relate to the words "betwixt" and "between". Whatever the origin of this curious local word, most Brightonians know about these intriguing pathways and the city is full of them (some nicer than others). It's even thought that it was once possible to walk from one side of Brighton's "Old Town" to the other, entirely through these curious alleyways.

Perhaps Brighton's most famous twitten, despite the fact that it's obscure and pretty derelict-looking, is tucked away behind Little East Street. It was nicknamed Quadrophenia Alley after being used as the location for the eponymous film's most famous scene. Read more on p. 84.

You'll find a nice walk that takes in each and every one of these twittens in the quirky Brighton guidebook, *Cheeky Walks*. It starts at St James's Street in Kemptown, then ventures across central Brighton up towards the station and the well-heeled area of Clifton. It's not to be rushed and takes around three hours, depending on how distracted you get along the way.

BRIGHTON TOY AND MODEL MUSEUM

An overlooked collection of toys

52–55 Trafalgar Street, Brighton BN1 4EB
Tel: 01273 749494
www.brightontoymuseum.co.uk
Open: Tues–Fri 10am–5pm, Sat 11am–5pm

Brighton is home to one of the world's finest collections of toys and models produced in the UK and Europe up until the mid-20th century, although most people don't know this.

The Brighton Toy and Model Museum, whose collection includes an extensive selection of trains, is fittingly housed inside four of the early Victorian arches underneath Brighton station, where it's been since 1991. Today, the 370sqm space is crammed with around 15,000 toys and models, packed into cabinets, which you browse to the sound of nostalgic jazz playing quietly in the background.

There are classic railway collections from Bing, Marklin and Bassett Lowke, soft toys, a huge selection of Meccano and other construction toys, thousands of Dinky, Matchbox and Corgi cars, not to mention puppets, dioramas, radio-controlled aircraft and old vintage arcade games.

This extraordinary collection was amassed by Chris Littledale, a man with an encyclopedic knowledge of toys. His interest was sparked by his father, a skilled model maker, and his mother, an avid collector of antiques. By the time he went to school, Chris had started gathering and restoring toys, and quickly amassed a grand and unique collection. Keen to share his love of toys with a wider audience, he founded the museum in 1990 together with a small group of friends, fellow collectors and model makers.

The museum's most treasured pieces are perhaps the two detailed working model railway layouts. One spans the back of the museum and showcases a detailed model of the Sussex countryside. The other forms the centrepiece of the museum, showing the layout of a typical British city in the 1930s, complete with original models, and three rails on which 50 trains (also dating back to the 1930s) run. Due to their age and value, the two model railway layouts are only fully operational twice a year (dates vary, so check the museum website for details).

A train-themed mural

On the museum's exterior wall, under the railway arches on Trafalgar Street, is a mural harking back to the days of steam. The mural was designed by the museum's founder, Chris Littledale, and was painted by local Brighton signwriter, Terry Smith.

SUSSEX MASONIC CENTRE

A hidden Art Deco gem

25 Queens Road, Brighton BN1 3YH
Tel: 01273 737404
http://sussexmasons.org.uk/articles/tour-the-sussex-masonic-centre
Open for private tours by prior arrangement with curator, Reg Barrow, and
during Heritage Open Days weekends: www.rth.org.uk/BHOD17
Admission free

The Sussex Masonic Centre, just two minutes from Brighton station, occupies a gigantic building spread across one block that most people walk past without noticing. However, behind this Regency façade is an Art Deco interior masterpiece designed by Brighton architect Samuel Denman. You can see inside on a tour with curator Reg Barrow.

Originally a private home built in the 1820s by the famous Regency architects Amon Wilds and Charles Busby, the building was lived in by various people, including the Kidds, a wealthy brewing family who moved here in 1862. In 1897 they bequeathed it to the Provincial Grand Lodge, who turned it into the Sussex Masonic Club, consisting of a bar and function rooms. A few years later, it was extended to provide further function and lodge rooms.

A visit starts in the original part of the building, which is still used as a social clubhouse today. Tucked behind the bar, albeit obscured by a coffee machine, is the foundation stone laid in 1901. However, the architectural magic arguably happens in the newer part of the building, starting at the entrance with its black-and-white chequerboard floor (found in all Masonic temples) and magnificent staircase, centred around an enormous brass and green-glass chandelier hanging from a stunning stained-glass skylight four floors above.

This part of the building was added in 1928, thanks to a generous donation of £9,000 from William Porter, a provincial grand senior warden designate of the time. Although the foundation stone was laid in 1919, the new extension wasn't finished and put into use until 1928, due to a delay in building work – allegedly down to a shortage of craftsman after the First World War.

The tour takes you up and around landings lined with cabinets and frames displaying all sorts of Masonic artefacts, from aprons and goblets to medals and photographs, and into impressive rooms. There's a huge dining room with space to host over 200 people, featuring original wood panelling and a beautiful minstrels' gallery. However, it's the main lodge room that's the most impressive (pictured). It's a grand affair, complete with another iconic black-and-white chequerboard floor and an unusual domed ceiling with a sun motif radiating out to signs of the zodiac.

LOAVES AND FISHES SCULPTURE

A modern work of art

Brighthelm Centre, North Road, Brighton BN1 1YD
www.brighthelm.org.uk

asily mistaken for a giant brutalist office block or car park, the Brighthelm building on the corner of North Road and Queens Road is actually a thriving community centre and modern church. Both play a major role in this area of the North Laine.

Despite the building's prominence, it's easy to miss the beautiful relief sculpture set into one of its low walls on North Road. This modern work of art, entitled *Loaves and Fishes*, is carved out of stone and depicts the parable of the Feeding of the Five Thousand. It was commissioned as part of the new building design and created by the late renowned sculptor John Skelton, who grew up in Sussex.

Many of Skelton's major works live on in cathedrals around the country, including St Paul's in London. His work was exhibited at the Royal Academy in London; the Brighton Festival; the huge Silver Jubilee Exhibition of Contemporary British Sculpture at Battersea Park in 1977; the Chelsea Harbour Sculpture Exhibition in 1993; the Tower Bridge Expo 1995; and, in 1993, a retrospective in his home town of Streat, for which he gathered more than 100 sculptures.

Remains of a forgotten chapel

Architect John Wells-Thorpe, who designed the new Hove Town Hall in Tisbury Road, was also responsible for the Brighthelm Centre. It was built in 1987 as part of an extension to the original Grade II-listed Hanover Chapel, dating back to 1825. Its intriguing southern façade, consisting of twin porches, Tuscan columns and giant pilasters, has been preserved and restored, and can be viewed at the back of the building.

Brighthelm Centre Community Garden

Also behind the Brighthelm Centre is a pretty community garden. It is home to 38 recorded tree specimens at last count, including Wych elms: these form part of Brighton's incredible National Elm Collection and can be discovered on the Brighton and Hove Elm Tree Trail (see p. 244). It's also a great example of a flourishing ecosystem, home to a wide range of local wildlife, including squirrels, bees, blackbirds and the occasional fox. Inside the centre, the Bright Now Café is open to the public (see p. 297).

JEW STREET

The forgotten centre of Brighton's Jewish heritage

Brighton BN1 1UT

3righton's first recorded Jewish resident was Israel Samuel, a silversmith, toymaker and lodging-house keeper, who arrived in 1776 when the place was still a fishing village. In March 2016 a plaque was put up outside his former home at No. 22 East Street, now home to the shop Crabtree & Evelyn. It was to mark Samuel's arrival, and to celebrate 250 years since the establishment of the Jewish community in Brighton and Hove and its contribution to the resort's growing success since its foundation.

Soon after Samuel arrived, the Jewish community started to develop in the North Laine area, around a narrow little alleyway called Jew Street. This is still in use today, albeit a little dingy and full of industrial-size rubbish bins.

According to local history records, Brighton's first synagogue was opened here as early as 1789 at the southern end of Jew Street. It was inside a rented building that would have been adapted as a synagogue at a time when the street had perhaps only three houses.

Physical remnants of this building can be found at what is now immediately behind No. 14 Bond Street. They include a curious bricked-up archway in the narrow passage leading from Jew Street to Bond Street, where the original synagogue entrance would have been.

Jewish contributions to the creation of Brighton are all around us in the city, not least architecturally. To name but a few examples: Sir Isaac Goldsmid, a director of the London, Brighton and South Coast Railway, was hugely influential in the development of the town; David Mocatta was the architect of Brighton railway station; Brighton Palace Pier was funded by Sir John Howard; Brighton Marina was conceived by Henry Cohen; the Middle Street Synagogue, opened in 1875, is often considered one of the city's most beautiful buildings (see p. 68); members of the Sassoon family established their own mausoleum in Paston Place (see p. 154); and David Marks is one half of the i360 team.

Today, Brighton's Jewish community is estimated at around 3,000, making it the fifth biggest Jewish community in the country. It is served by four synagogues.

THE OLD VICARAGE

The only house on the high street

87 London Road, Brighton BN1 4JF

ondon Road might have been hailed as the country's "new Shoreditch" for its recent gentrification, which has seen quirky cafés and refurbished pubs and shops spring up overnight. However, there is one building that stands out, albeit subtly, from the crowd. It strikes a nostalgic chord that reminds us of the city's architectural heritage.

Sandwiched between the oversized Alcampo Lounge café-bar and what was once a Methodist church is a timeworn gem of historic architecture – a double-fronted house. It happens to be the only remaining single-family residential property in the road. The Regency Society founder, Dr Antony Dale, described it as "the finest individual Regency house in the city".

It's thought to have been designed and built in 1825 by well-known Regency architects Charles Busby and Amon Wilds. Originally called Arundel Place, it was designed as a residence for a man called Nathaniel Cooke Jr, who worked as an organist, music teacher and composer.

After Cooke moved out, the house was used as a school called Cambridge Lodge, where John Ackerson Erredge – a well-known local historian and author – is believed to have taught. In around 1866, the name was changed to Cambridge Cottage, but by the 1890s it had been changed back to Cambridge Lodge, although no one knows why.

Today, it's often referred to as "the Old Vicarage" or "St Bartholomew's Vicarage", alluding to the time it was used as the clergy house for the vicar of St Bartholomew's Church (see p. 186), although the church is said to have sold it off in the 1970s.

Today, it's a private residence, so you can't go inside for a nose around. But you can take a minute to stop outside and admire the elegant, ornate façade, including a beautiful round-arched entrance surrounded by a stunning ironwork porch.

In 2011 The Regency Society published a story in its newsletter raising concerns about the building's condition – the society claimed that Brighton & Hove City Council's heritage team had promised to monitor this. However, in 2014, the building was included in an article on *The Argus* website with the headline, "Architectural gems that need to be saved before it is too late", so its future remains unsure.

FORMER ISETTA FACTORY SITE

Birthplace of the "bubble car"…

27 New England Street, Brighton BN1 4CQ

A small blue oval plaque outside Sainsbury's, above a row of bicycle racks, alerts passers-by to the fact that, from 1957 to 1964, this was the site of the BMW Isetta factory in the former Brighton Locomotive Works.

The Isetta was a tiny bubble-shaped car with one door and three wheels, first manufactured in 1953 by an Italian firm called Iso. BMW bought the rights to manufacture the car in Great Britain, setting up shop six weeks after the locomotive works closed. Over eight years, 30,000 Isettas were built at the factory by its 200-odd staff, most of whom had worked on railway vehicles at the former locomotive works. Output started at 90 a week and increased to 300 at its peak.

Set at the top of a steep hill without direct access to a main road, it wasn't the most practical site for a car-manufacturing plant. Parts were shipped into the yard and the finished product carried out on flat wagons that ran on existing railway tracks on the factory floor.

The factory was demolished in 1969 and the site turned into a 900-capacity car park, which closed some time in the 1990s. It then became part of what was once the largest derelict area in Brighton. This was eventually absorbed by New England Square as part of the New England Quarter development, where you'll find Sainsbury's.

The plaque was presented by the Isetta Owners' Club of Great Britain to mark the site. It was unveiled in 2003 by Leonard White, a former worker at the factory.

The Isetta was made under licence in a number of different countries around the world during the late 1950s and early 1960s, with BMW using their existing motorbike technology to re-engineer the car. According to a 1960 article in the *Brighton Herald*, the Isetta ran on 60 miles to the gallon, cost £320 to buy and was the first cabin scooter to be manufactured in Great Britain. As it had only three wheels, you only needed a motorcycle licence to drive one. Due to its shape, it became known as the "bubble car", a name later given to other similar-style cars.

SILVER ALTAR

A special feature hidden inside the country's tallest church

St Bartholomew's Church, Ann Street, Brighton BN1 4GP
www.stbartholomewsbrighton.org.uk/welcome.htm
Open: Mon–Sat 10am–1pm, 2pm–4.30pm for visitors and prayer, as well as Sunday services
Admission free

St Bart's is allegedly Britain's biggest church, a gargantuan Italianate Gothic structure made completely out of brick. It is 55 metres long, 18 metres wide and 43 metres high, to the top of the gilt metal cross, making it 1.2 metres taller than Westminster Abbey.

The church is so tall, it can be seen from almost wherever you are in the city. Even when you step inside, it's easy to be transfixed by the sheer size of the nave and the marble decorations, but be sure not to miss some of the smaller, more curious details, particularly a magnificent silver altar on the east side.

Added in 1902 by the church's interior designer Henry Wilson to replace the original altar, the new one is particularly intriguing for the metalwork detailing on the front. This shows a sun and the Assyrian symbols of the planets: Saturn is a scorpion, Mercury is a serpent, Mars is a wolf, Jupiter is a thunderbolt in a fist, Venus is an owl and a lion symbolises the sun. There's also a beautiful silver lamp hanging over it, said to date back to the 15th century and to have come from Russia.

Other notable features include the stunning, well-documented high altar at the far end, reached by marble steps and covered by a 14-metre Byzantine-style red and green marble baldacchino. There's also a beautiful gold mosaic and mother-of-pearl ceiling; a pulpit consisting of six red marble columns on a black marble base, supporting a large block of green Irish marble; and a silver altar backed by mosaics designed by Frederick Hamilton Jackson beneath a towering crucifix.

Four confessionals are scattered around the church – look out for their oriental-style, onion-shaped domes.

The church was designed in 1874 by local architect, Edmund Scott, for Arthur Douglas Wagner. This wealthy vicar was responsible for building several churches in the poorest areas of Brighton and paying for them from his own pocket.

Concerts at St Bartholomew's

With its unique acoustics and size, St Bartholomew's is the ideal venue for concerts, which are held there during the Brighton Festival in May. It also hosts various other orchestral and choral concerts throughout the year, including regular appearances by the Sussex Symphony Orchestra, the Sussex Chorus, the Brighton Symphony Orchestra and the Brighton Youth Orchestra. Visit www.brightonfestival.org and check out the "What's On" section.

THE GARDEN HOUSE

A market garden in the heart of the city

5 Warleigh Road, Brighton BN1 4NT
Tel: 07788 668595 or 07729 037182
www.gardenhousebrighton.co.uk
Open: May–Sept, by arrangement, for various events and courses

Behind a row of terraced townhouses, close to the Round Hill area of Brighton, is a remarkable, sprawling secret garden. Originally a Victorian market garden, today it's an inspirational oasis where people can come to learn about gardening. It's also open occasionally to the public for charity events.

"The garden wasn't always so beautiful," says owner Bridgette Saunders, a horticulturalist and teacher who bought the house and garden with her husband 18 years ago, and propagates most of the plants herself. "It was in such a terrible state, completely overgrown and filled with junk. It took us two years to clear the rubble and turn it into something that resembled a garden, so it's been a labour of love from the start!"

Together with her business partner Deborah Kalinke, a garden designer, Bridgette runs a regular weekly session at The Garden House called The Friday Group, when 25 people gather together to garden, chat and learn gardening techniques. Their goal: to prepare the garden for local charity open days, which they host a few times each year.

There's so much to discover on a wander around – a vegetable patch, a stunning cut-flower garden, fruit trees, container plants, old climbing roses and a pond. Not forgetting a greenhouse, a compost and propagation area, places to sit, and the odd piece of local artwork, such as mosaics and sculptures.

Today, The Garden House has become more than a place to learn gardening. It offers courses, talks, visits and workshops – for the enthusiastic amateur and the more experienced gardener. It also organises garden-focused trips further afield, to places such as Cape Town, Berlin, Norfolk, Madeira and Japan.

The ideal venue for supper clubs and dinner parties

Bridgette and Deborah recently added a dedicated "garden studio" hidden among the trees – a large teaching space, complete with wood-burning stove, which can comfortably hold courses for up to 25 people, all year round, and makes the ideal venue for supper clubs and dinner parties.

MAX MILLER ROOM

A secret museum in a back-street chippy

Bardsley's of Baker Street, 22–23a Baker Street, Brighton BN1 4JN
Tel: 01273 681256
http://maxmiller.org/museum.html
Open: Tues–Sat. Lunch 12pm–3pm (last orders 2.30pm); dinner 4.30pm–
9.30pm (last orders 9pm)

Ⓞne of Brighton's oldest and best-loved fish and chip shops is the setting for a "secret" museum of rare original memorabilia. The collection celebrates the life and career of Max Miller, Brighton's famous music-hall star known as the "Cheeky Chappie" (see p. 74).

So before you tuck into a plate of Brighton's finest fish and chips in Bardsley's dining room, take some time to notice the original film posters, music-hall bills and photographs of Max Miller, the "pure gold of the music hall".

The collection was developed in collaboration with the Max Miller Appreciation Society, founded by a group of fans in 1999 to keep his memory alive. It was opened at Bardsley's in 2009 by the society's patron, Michael Aspel.

Born in Brighton, Miller was considered one of Britain's top comedians in the 1930s, 40s and 50s. He excelled as a stand-up comic, playing in large variety theatres. Miller was considered a master of the double entendre, earning him the nickname "Cheeky Chappie". His style was mischievous, brash and quick-witted and he wore loud, over-the-top costumes.

Before the collection found a permanent home at Bardsley's, the society's collection of memorabilia first went on display at the Brighton Museum and Art Gallery. The exhibition was opened in 2003 by Brighton-based English actress, Dora Bryan, and American musician, Carol Kaye. It was originally displayed in a separate room in Bardsley's but has recently been relocated to the main dining room.

One of Brighton's longest-surviving family-run restaurants

Bardsley's of Baker Street is unusual in itself in that it's one of the city's oldest surviving restaurants – it opened in 1926. It has been run by four generations of the same family ever since. It was founded by great-grandfather, Ben Bardsley, a blacksmith from Lancashire who moved to Brighton during the Depression. He opened the first Bardsley's shop in Upper Russell Street, where the Churchill Shopping Centre now stands. This became the first in a chain of Bardsley family-owned chippies around town at one point. Today, Bardsley's of Baker Street is the only one remaining, keeping the family tradition alive, but it's still going strong.

IRELAND'S GARDENS GATEWAY

Remains of a pleasure garden

Union Road, Brighton BN1

cross the street from the north end of The Level, on the outskirts of Brighton's Round Hill area, is a forgotten-looking set of iron gates flanked by two concrete pillars topped by lions. This once grand opening marked the entrance to a stately, yet short-lived venture known as Ireland's Pleasure Gardens or the Royal Pleasure Gardens.

James Ireland, a prosperous woollen draper and undertaker, commissioned the pleasure gardens, hoping to cash in on Brighton's growing popularity as a seaside destination. He wanted to attract the increasing number of visitors and short-term residents, which had doubled the city's population over the previous decade.

Ireland bought the 10-acre (4-hectare) site in 1822 from the developer of Kemp Town, Thomas Read Kemp, and opened the impressive pleasure gardens on 1 May 1823. The site had an aviary maze, formal gardens with a canal, a Gothic-style tower, bowling greens, billiard rooms, assembly rooms with a roof garden, a grotto, a lake and a cricket ground – said to be the best in the country. Ireland is even believed to have planned high-profile stunts, like flying demonstrations.

But despite his efforts, the gardens never thrived and soon fell into decline. Ireland sold them in 1826, with later owners presiding over further decline until the facility was eventually closed in the 1840s.

Only the gardens' south boundary wall, and the gate piers decorated with copies of their original stone lions, survive. However, people living in the Park Crescent Estate get to enjoy the extensive gardens.

NEARBY

Round Hill cats' creep

An intriguing feature of the Round Hill area is what's known as a "cats' creep", a local term like "twitten" (see p. 172): this refers to a steep, narrow staircase between buildings, mostly found in Brighton's steep suburbs, such as Hollingbury. There is a nice example in Lennox Place, between Roundhill Crescent and Richmond Road. It was originally designed as a residential street with houses on it. However, it was too steep for horses and carts, so it became a footpath with eight flights of 15 steps instead. It's now a popular shortcut.

SHOE TREE

An old elm tree full of trainers

Sensory Garden, The Level, Union Road, Brighton BN2 9SY

Once the Prince Regent's cricket ground, The Level is now one of the city's busiest parks, well known for its recent £2 million renovation and new skate park, which attracts skaters from all over the South-East. However, there's a more unusual and unexpected sight tucked away in a quiet leafy area in the southern part of the park known as the Sensory Garden: dozens of trainers – mainly skate shoes – hanging from the branches of an old elm tree.

When the shoes started appearing in 2010, passers-by were left wondering how they got there. Some think it started as a prank; others suggest it could be a memorial to someone, a meeting point for drug dealers, an unofficial art installation – much like the Flint Grotto on the beach (see p. 36) – or simply just another of the city's quirky sights.

It's also been suggested that it's the work of skateboarders who prefer to fling their worn-out skate shoes into a tree rather than throw them away. Or – the most extreme scenario – it's a nod to the US, where it's a gang-culture tradition to throw shoes into a tree or over a telephone wire when a gang member is killed …

A 2015 video report by Brighton's *Latest News* channel claimed to have solved the mystery, revealing that the shoes are thrown up into the tree as a mark of support for the park by skaters who use it. Whether this is true or not, no one knows.

Discovering the little-known Sensory Garden

The Sensory Garden is often overlooked by people visiting the The Level in favour of the skate park and children's playground. However, as well as the "shoe tree", it's home to a fabulous games area, including a *pétanque* ground lined with artist-designed chess tables. *Pétanque* is a French game where the goal is to toss or roll hollow steel balls as close as possible to a small wooden ball called a *cochonnet*, or jack, while standing inside a circle with both feet on the ground. On weekdays, you can borrow a set of balls or chess pieces and a timer clock free of charge from the garden manager and enjoy a game. You'll find another *pétanque* ground near the Peace Statue (see p. 14).

BENJAMIN JAMES SMITH HOUSE

A carefully curated ode to the Georgian period …

North Laine, Brighton
Open for tours on the last Thursday and Friday of each month only by
arrangement (via email) with the owner: wallis.harper.49@gmail.com

Nothing distinguishes Benjamin James Smith House from its whitewashed North Laine cottage counterparts except perhaps the curious brass door furniture – which also acts as a little hint of what's to come.

Stepping through the front door, however, you couldn't feel further removed from the uniformity of the street and the buzz of contemporary Brighton as you emerge in a Georgian-style time-capsule home … not a piece of 21st-century technology in sight.

This carefully curated interior, named after the property's first owner, belongs to Craig, an American antique collector with a passion for British history and interior design. He moved to Brighton in the 1970s, bought the property in the late 80s and has spent almost the past three decades masterfully creating what we see today, although making sure to avoid "the coldness of perfection".

"I grew up in New Jersey in the 1950s when everything was shiny and new, but I was always more interested in knights and castles. I also love looking inside other people's houses and am fascinated by how people in history live," says Craig. He offers private tours of his home, with plenty of stories and anecdotes along the way. Tours start in the basement, with its magnificent cosy drawing room painted a soft canary yellow, a reminder of a similar room in one of Craig's favourite style inspirations: the Sir John Soane's Museum in London's Lincoln's Inn Fields.

A walk around Benjamin James Smith House is a mesmerising experience. The place is crammed, yet doesn't feel cluttered at all, despite every wall and surface being filled with collections of antique finds, including an extensive collection of portrait paintings.

There's also the odd, quirky personal addition, such as a vintage map of Manhattan on the kitchen wall (a nod to Craig's homeland), a wonderful enamel 1951 Tricity cooker complete with Bakelite knobs (here when Craig moved in) and a wall clock dating back to the 1800s. Craig discovered the clock in a local flea market and it just happens to be made by local clockmaker, James Rich, whose studio once occupied the basement.

"I used to be editing constantly, swapping pieces for things I found more perfect, but I'm now cautious about introducing anything new," says Craig. "Everything has been in place for a while, and it's reached a point where I love everything dearly and there's a nice balance and stillness."

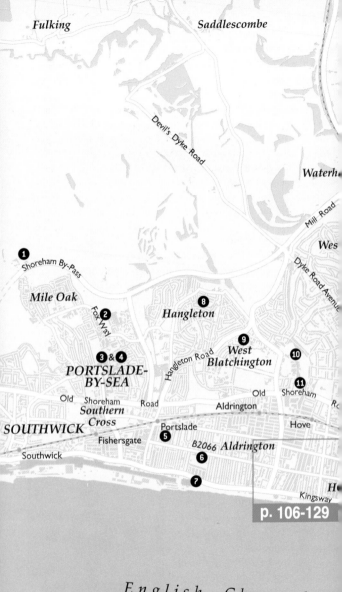

Fulking

Saddlescombe

Devil's Dyke Road

Waterh

Mill Road

Wes

Dyke Road Avenue

1 Shoreham By-Pass

Mile Oak

Fox Way

2

8

Hangleton

3 & 4

**PORTSLADE-
BY-SEA**

Hangleton Road

9

*West
Blatchington*

10

11

Shoreham

Old

Shoreham   Road

Southern
Cross

Old
Aldrington

Ro

SOUTHWICK

Cross

Hove

Portslade

5

Fishersgate

B2066   *Aldrington*

6

Southwick

7

H

Kingsway

p. 106-129

English   Channel

0   1 km   2 km

Hove Park to Portslade

① MILE OAK FARM 200

② FOREDOWN TOWER 202

③ PORTSLADE MANOR RUINS 204

④ ST MARYE'S CONVENT BURIAL GROUND 206

⑤ SECRET GARDEN 208

⑥ DINO THE ELEPHANT SCULPTURE 210

⑦ HOVE LAGOON MODEL YACHT CLUB 212

⑧ THE CIRCUS PROJECT 214

⑨ WEST BLATCHINGTON WINDMILL 216

⑩ HOVE PARK MINIATURE RAILWAY 218

⑪ THE GOLDSTONE 220

MILE OAK FARM

Brighton's "city farm"

Mile Oak Road, Portslade, Brighton BN41 2RF
Tel: 01273 424651
www.mileoakfarm.co.uk
Open: Mon–Sat 9am–5pm, Sun 10am–4pm

Although Brighton is surrounded by the endless rolling hills of the South Downs National Park, providing plenty of opportunities to see animals on farms, there's a "city farm" much closer to home.

Mile Oak Farm is located on the fringes of Hove, just behind the area of Portslade. This 445-hectare family farm has been managed by the Cross family for three generations.

It started out as a dairy farm, but has reinvented itself over the years to keep up with the times. The Crosses eventually sold their dairy herd and opened a farm shop, which originally sold horse feed for the 30 or so horse liveries at the farm. Over the years, it has expanded to introduce new lines and include better facilities, such as family attractions.

There are all the typical farmyard animals to see – from chickens, ducks and goats to peacocks. Children can also enjoy donkey rides at certain times during the weekend.

To remind you of your trip, the farm shop is bursting with delicious local produce to take home, including locally grown fresh fruit and vegetables, meat and pies from a local butcher, and honey produced on the farm. There's also a tearoom serving drinks and homemade cakes.

The converted dairy building at Mile Oak Farm is where the quirky, nostalgic Gran Stead's Ginger Co. produces its non-alcoholic ginger drinks and traditional lemonade – also for sale in the farm shop. Visit www.gransteadsginger.co.uk for more information.

East Sussex family farms

There are lots of family farms around Brighton. Saddlescombe Farm, 8 km north of the city (www.camillaandroly.co.uk/saddlescombe-farm), offers farm visits, courses for aspiring shepherds, a backpackers' campsite and lambing open days. Blackberry Farm Park (www.blackberry-farm.co.uk), near Lewes, puts on tractor and pony rides. You can pick your own fruit and veg at Sharnfold Farm (www.sharnfoldfarm.co.uk). Heaven Farm (heavenfarm.co.uk) has friendly wallabies and a bluebell nature trail. Middle Farm (www.middlefarm.com) has all your farmyard favourites and a farm shop.

FOREDOWN TOWER

Home of one of the world's largest working camera obscuras

Foredown Road, Portslade, Brighton BN41 2EW
Tel: 01273 415625
www.portslade.org/foredown-tower/
Café and viewing gallery: Mon–Fri 10am–2pm
Camera obscura demonstrations: every Tues, Thurs and last Sat of the month
at 11am, 12 noon and 1pm (additionally, 2pm on Sat only)

The i360 isn't the only attraction in Brighton and Hove to offer a dramatic bird's-eye panoramic view over Sussex. Perched on the South Downs outside central Hove is a more old-fashioned, eccentric option.

The Foredown Tower was built in 1909 to house a heavy cast-iron water tank that served the old Hangleton isolation hospital. Today, this beautiful Edwardian structure has been converted into a countryside centre, home to hands-on displays telling the story of the landscape and one of the largest operational camera obscuras in the world – a unique optical device used to observe the surrounding landscape, sun and sky.

The history of the camera obscura dates as far back as the Renaissance. These cameras were popular in Victorian times, especially at the seaside. Portable versions were introduced in the 17th century and became popular with artists, who used them as an aide to accurate drawing and to document their travels. In fact, Josiah Wedgwood, the famous potter, is known to have used one to draw views to decorate some of his pottery.

Originally made for the Gateshead Garden Festival, the one you see at Foredown is one of two working camera obscuras in the South-East. It has a field of vision nearly three times greater than average-sized binoculars, a 12-inch (30.48 cm) diameter lens and a focal length of 18 ft (5.49 metres).

During the demonstration, you get to spot local landmarks projected on a screen below and if you're lucky, on a clear day, you'll be able to see as far as the Isle of Wight.

If you visit on a day the camera isn't in operation, the top floor is still open as a viewing gallery. The tower is also the starting point for four circular walking routes: the Devil's Dyke railway line trail, St Helen's Church, Hangleton Manor and Dovecote – details of which are available inside.

The flint walls running along two of the tower's sides are all that survive of the old isolation hospital that stood where the neighbouring housing estate is located today. The hospital took care of patients with infectious diseases for 100 years until medical advances forced it to close in the 1980s.

PORTSLADE MANOR RUINS

Brighton's oldest curiosity

Emmaus, Drove Road, Portslade Village BN41 2PA
Open: Mon–Sat 9.30am–5pm, when Emmaus is open to the public

The grand bow-fronted Georgian property known as Portslade's "new" manor house was built in 1807 and was privately owned until 1904, when it became a convent. Today, it's home to Emmaus, a branch of the worldwide charity that provides work and lodgings for the long-term homeless and unemployed. Hidden within the grounds is possibly Brighton's most ancient curiosity – some Norman ruins.

The new manor was built to replace an old Norman manor house, some of whose remains you'll find in the Emmaus market garden, along with others which can be seen if you peek through the fence next to the community allotment.

The oldest part of the original manor house dates back to the early 12th century, making it one of the very few surviving ruins of a Norman manor in the country. It was recently declared a Scheduled Ancient Monument and given Grade II listing.

The manor originally had two storeys and a basement, part of which sits above ground. It was originally twice the size, as can be seen today from what remains. Over the centuries, the building was extended and altered at various times: the western part dates from around 1611, while the main part of the house – although it's now gone – was still standing in 1802. If you look carefully to the left of the entrance, you can see where another wall once joined.

When the new structure was built, the old Portslade Manor was briefly used as an almshouse for the poor until it was demolished to form a garden folly. The real reason for its destruction is not known, although it's rumoured to be down to a family dispute.

A deserted graveyard

Across the road from Emmaus is a delightfully overgrown woodland, home to a deserted graveyard once used by the nuns who lived here when the building was a convent (see following double-page spread).

It's not widely known that Emmaus is home to a thrift superstore and the Greenhouse garden shop in the conservatory, which is jam-packed full of gardening ephemera. There's also a café serving breakfast, lunch and drinks, which you can enjoy outside in the vegetable garden while you say hello to the chickens, see p.207 for more details.

ST MARYE'S CONVENT BURIAL GROUND

The underground gateway to a secret graveyard

Emmaus, Drove Road, Portslade Village BN41 2PA
Open occasionally for special events
For latest news, visit www.facebook.com/Emmausbrighton/

The Norman ruins of the old Portslade Manor aren't the only curiosity hidden in the grounds of the "new" Portslade Manor (1807), which currently houses the Brighton branch of the global homeless charity, Emmaus (see p. 204). Across the road, accessed by an intriguing ivy-clad tunnel, is the gated entrance to a curious old burial ground that most people in Brighton and Hove don't know exists.

You can't wander inside for a look-around as it's currently kept under lock and key, but if you walk to the end of the tunnel, you can take a peek through a timeworn arched gated entrance.

Although at first glance it looks abandoned and overgrown, this is in fact the delightful setting for a secret graveyard and woodland. The new Portslade Manor was the home of St Marye's Convent in the early 1900s, well before Emmaus set up home here in 1997. The nuns who once lived here still occasionally use it for burials.

Today, it's affectionately known as the "Emmaus secret garden". Although it remains closed, except for the occasional burial, and is rarely used, it's open to the public for the odd special event. Emmaus has exciting plans to make more use of it – including the opportunity for people to visit and see inside it. Details will be posted on the Emmaus Facebook page – see the link on the opposite page.

A little known flea market

While you're here, don't miss a trip to the Emmaus Secondhand Superstore, one of the biggest flea markets in Brighton – most people living in the city centre don't even know of its existence. It's located on the site of the former convent laundry and is home to a huge vintage and thrift shop called The Emporium, filled with all kinds of retro, collectable, handmade and upcycled goods, and a quirky gardening shop called The Greenhouse in the conservatory. This is stocked with gardening ephemera mostly donated by the public, from terracotta pots and ceramic planters, garden furniture and recliners, to gardening tools, books, house plants and garden gnomes. What was once the convent's dining room is home to the little-known Revive Café, which serves breakfasts, lunches and drinks – you can enjoy them outside in the vegetable garden while you say hello to the chickens.

SECRET GARDEN

A community garden in an abandoned churchyard

St Leonard's Church, New Church Road, Hove BN3 4ED
Open 24/7

Follow the path lined with moss-covered gravestones, round to the left of St Leonard's Church, and you'll discover a delightful award-winning community garden. With its abundant wildflower beds, pond, beehives and vegetable plots, it's hard to believe it was once abandoned, swallowed up under 2 metres of nettles after 14 years of neglect.

Today, it's a magical community garden open 24 hours a day, seven days a week, for everyone to enjoy. "We encourage people of all age groups to visit and get involved, from young children to the elderly, of all abilities, even if you just want to come and have a chat," says the secretary, Joi Jones. She is part of the team responsible for transforming this once-abandoned wilderness of brambles, nettles and weeds into an award-winning community venture.

The project began in 2013, when the vicar of St Leonard's put out a request for a group of people to manage an overgrown plot of land at the rear of the graveyard.

"A small group of interested gardeners – including me – took up the challenge and we've since won a 2017 South & South East in Bloom award in the 'community garden' category," says Joi. A meander around reveals a bounty of natural delights – the pond filled with frogs and newts, a vegetable and herb garden, raised beds bursting with flowers and plants, and an enchanting scented area.

There's also a greenhouse and large potting shed, a wildlife area where you'll find a hedgehog house and monitoring tunnel, nests of slowworms, resident blackbirds, robins, sparrows and great-tits and an apiary with four honey-bee colonies," adds Joi. "Our mantra is to be as organic as possible in our approach, allowing natural predators to control pests and diseases."

The Secret Garden volunteer team gathers every Wednesday and Saturday from 11am to 3pm and relies on voluntary donations to continue making improvements and maintaining the space. The group is always interested in hearing from new volunteers.

An ideal spot for summer gatherings and tea parties

The Secret Garden occasionally hosts events. In 2016, it was transformed into a 1940s-style garden tea party for the Queen's 90th birthday celebrations, which saw a large turn-out of Hove locals. The following year, it held a strawberry festival. To find out more, visit its Facebook page: https://www.facebook.com/secretgardengrouphove/

DINO THE ELEPHANT SCULPTURE

An ode to Hove's forgotten travelling circus elephant

Wish Park, Wish Road, Marine Avenue, Hove BN3 4LH
www.brighton-hove.gov.uk/venue/wish-park

Legend has it that travelling circuses used to visit Hove frequently: according to a local tale, a travelling circus elephant was buried in the south-west corner of Wish Park after it died during a performance here.

To commemorate this intriguing snippet of local history, over in the children's play area, you'll find an eye-catching sculpture in the shape of an elephant's rib cage, which also conveniently doubles up as a shelter and seating area.

Designed by a local company called Chalk Architecture, the sculpture was commissioned following a competition run by Brighton & Hove City Council in collaboration with the Friends of Wish Park and families from the local community. It has glulam-wood "ribs" (a strong, light and durable material) and is partially clad with recycled pier decking, which is also used for the bench.

As part of the winning bid and to involve the community, award-winning local creative director, Richard Wolfströme, invited local children to participate in a poetry-writing workshop: the children were asked to create haiku-type and two-word kenning poems about elephants. Working with the children's material, Richard then laser-etched their words into the pier-deck cladding sections – haikus on the outside, kennings on the inside.

"Sometimes it not always the 'big' projects with all the kudos that can bring the most satisfaction," says Richard. "This is one of my own personal favourite projects. It took huge commitment and everyone working together to see this one through. Not only is the structure beautiful – it is the community intention and work behind it. And then to read all the wonderful poems just makes my heart smile," he adds.

The sculpture was named *Dino the Elephant* following a competition organised by Brighton & Hove City Council which was won by Willa Hornsey. It was officially opened by the Mayor of Brighton, Pete West, on 29 October 2016.

HOVE LAGOON MODEL YACHT CLUB

A secret sailing society

Hove Lagoon, Kingsway, Hove BN3 4LX
Tel: 01273 264592
https://hovelagoonmyc.wikispaces.com/home
Open: March–Nov, every Sunday, 9.30am–2pm

Hove Lagoon is no secret to the people of Brighton and Hove, well known as the city's go-to venue for all kinds of watersports, such as windsurfing, cable-tow wakeboarding and sailing – and the location for Brighton resident DJ Fatboy Slim's Big Beach Café. What's less well known is that it's home to Brighton's only model yacht club. Not only that: the club has been around since 1929 and started sailing boats when the lagoon opened in 1930. Model yachts have sailed on its waters continuously since then, with only a break for the Second World War.

The club is still going strong today. Members meet every Sunday morning (from March to November) to race two different types of model yacht. There is "an Australian member who sails a boat named *Kate and Sydney* and a Dutchman with his boat *Dutch Courage*, which makes for some interesting banter," says club secretary, Les Baker. "To keep members on their toes and test skills, there are also seven trophy races held each year."

The Hove Lagoon Model Yacht Club has 25 members and welcomes visitors from other clubs and anyone wanting to have a go. "We are always looking for more people to join us, especially some not as long in the tooth as many of us!" Les adds.

Brighton & Hove City Council – then the Brighton Corporation – bought Hove Lagoon from a private owner in 1896 and turned it into a watersports lagoon for public use, which opened in 1930, the layout much the same then as it is today.

During the Second World War, Hove Lagoon was used as a training ground in the run-up to D-Day – along with the rest of the seafront – which saw tanks tested at night to make sure they were watertight.

NEARBY

Hove Lagoon Nature Corridor

Just in front of Hove Lagoon near the main road, you'll spot a long grassy strip. This is set to become a nature corridor, which will feature a butterfly hotel, "particularly for our winged visitors from France who are pretty exhausted once they have flown over the English Channel", says Lucy Williams, part of the project design team (see also Regency Dragonflies, p. 260). "We hope particularly to attract the Swallowtail and the Brighton Argus (also known as the Long-Tailed Blue) butterflies," she says. The corridor, which will also feature a series of butterfly-inspired sculptures dotted along the bank, is set to open in 2018.

THE CIRCUS PROJECT

Circus-based activities boost confidence by encouraging risk-taking in a safe environment

Hangleton Community Centre, 1 Harmsworth Crescent, Hove BN3 8BW
Tel: 01273 739106
www.thecircusproject.co.uk
Open for classes and performances only: see website

Concealed behind the conventional façade of an ordinary community centre is the setting for an exciting and unconventional activity.

Founded in 1999, the award-winning Circus Project is where aspiring acrobats and trapeze artists can hone their skills in an energetic and fun environment, using professional circus equipment. Specialising in aerial circus, the project runs weekly classes, giving children and adults the opportunity to explore a wide range of aerial equipment, including the static trapeze, rope and silks. There are also ground-based circus activities like poi, hula hoop, walking the tight rope and acrobalance/creating human pyramids.

The project's artistic director, Vicki McManus, trained at The National Centre for Circus Arts in London, specialising in aerial techniques, trapeze, rope and silks. She has performed all over the world in theatre, circus shows, cabaret, adverts and opening ceremonies, including the London 2012 Olympic Games.

"Everyone is welcome to participate in The Circus Project regardless of age, gender and ability," says Vicki. "We aim to be an inclusive activity: all are welcome to try. We run a youth programme for children aged 7 and over throughout the year as well as weekly adult classes for beginners to advanced. We are also planning to start pre-school classes for parents or carers and their children."

Vicki has witnessed first-hand the positive effect that circus arts have on an individual: "Although it might seem scary, taking part in circus-based activities boosts confidence by encouraging risk-taking in a safe environment, and gives a sense of personal achievement and belonging."

The project also runs a successful youth circus programme, a group of highly skilled young circus artists aged 14–19 who have represented the UK at various circus festivals around the world, and performed original circus theatre shows all over the UK.

According to Vicki, "Some of our youth students are now working as professional aerial artists, training at Circomedia in Bristol and working at Camp America for the summer teaching aerial circus."

At grass-roots level, the project also runs weekly training sessions for over 70 local children, who get to perform shows and cabarets at Hangleton Community Centre, where the project is based.

WEST BLATCHINGTON WINDMILL ⑨

A museum in a windmill

191 Holmes Avenue, Hove BN3 7LH
www.sussexmillsgroup.org.uk/blatchington.htm
Open: May–Sept on Sundays and Bank Holidays, 2.30pm–5pm; and on
National Mills Weekend, 11am–5pm. See www.nationalmillsweekend.co.uk

West Blatchington Windmill is one of many windmills in the Brighton area. Built around 1820, it was beautifully painted by John Constable in a watercolour dated 5 November 1825. Although it's an ordinary "smock"-style mill – named after the garment worn by millers and shepherds of the time – this one stands out for its design. At the time, it was considered somewhat of a curiosity because of its hexagonal rather than traditional octagonal form. It's now a quirky museum of milling, open to the public throughout the summer.

The mill was originally built to provide flour and animal feeds for Court Farm, which no longer exists. It was forced to close in 1897 after its fans – or "sweeps" as they're known in Sussex – broke during a catastrophic storm, although remarkably all the original milling machinery remained intact. Hove Council bought the mill in the 1930s, but it wasn't until the 1970s that, with the help of a group of volunteers, it was extensively renovated and restored.

The museum is spread across all six floors. Here visitors can learn the story of the mill, find out more about how a mill actually works and browse all the original machinery on display throughout.

A quirky voting venue

On 7 May 2015, the windmill was used as a polling station for Hove Constituency in the General Election.

A private collector in the United States owns Constable's painting of the mill. In 1993 it was flown back to England especially so that it could appear in an exhibition entitled *The Romantic Windmill*, organised by curator Tim Wilcox at Hove Museum (see p. 108).

A smugglers' rest

Rumour has it that West Blatchington Windmill is strongly associated with smuggling. This is mainly because it would have made a good seamark for smugglers arriving from France, but also because it was once close to a well-known landing beach at the foot of Hove Street. It is thought that the smugglers brought brandy and tobacco into the mill hidden in carts loaded with fishermen's tackle; this included those bulky, fibrous fenders normally placed between boats and landing stages, which could be hollowed out to hide contraband.

HOVE PARK MINIATURE RAILWAY

An ode to the golden age of train travel

Hove Park, Goldstone Crescent, Hove BN3 6LX
www.hoveparkrailway.co.uk
Open: March–Oct, check website for details

Tucked away in the north-west corner of this popular family park in Hove is a fascinating hidden gem dating back to the 1950s: a 610-metre-long miniature railway. You can either watch it in action or enjoy a ride on it, which takes you around the whole track and even through a tunnel.

This ode to the golden age of train travel is run by a band of enthusiastic, steam-loving volunteers known as the Hove Park Railway Society. They enjoy getting together to build, maintain and run steam, electric and all sorts of other model forms of transportation – for the enjoyment of the public as well as themselves.

Most of the locomotives and equipment used on the railway are built by the society's members in their own workshops, including an entire set of new carriages installed in 2017 to replace the original ones that were 20 years old.

The railway was initially set up at Withdean Zoo – now closed – and started out as a single, short "up and down" raised track laid to 2.5-inch, 3.5-inch and 5-inch gauges. In 1951 it was moved and installed in Hove Park at the side of the old Victorian pumping station (now the British Engineerium) and officially opened by the mayor.

The scheme was an immediate success, with over 500 passengers carried on the official opening day. In 1957 the railway was expanded to include a second track running parallel to the original, both of which were extended to a length of 82.3 metres.

Not far from the miniature railway is a fascinating piece of public art called Fingermaze by environmental artist Chris Drury (www.chrisdrury.co.uk). It's designed to resemble the shape of a giant's fingerprint with a maze pattern at the centre. The installation is made of York flagstone and lime mortar, and has weathered over time as it's aged, blurring into the landscape.

Just inside the entrance to Hove Park you'll notice a giant stone set within a fenced-off area. It's thought that this stone once formed part of Sussex's ancient stone circle (see p. 220).

THE GOLDSTONE

An ancient relic in a family park

Hove Park, Goldstone Crescent, Hove BN3 6BG

Just inside the entrance to Hove Park is a mysterious giant lump of sandstone and flint, sprinkled with flecks of gold throughout, which gives this piece of geology its name: the Goldstone.

Local legend suggests the Devil kicked it here in anger after stubbing his toe on it, while digging a trench that would force the sea to flood in and destroy all the churches sheltering in the South Downs. The trench-digging project was abandoned, leaving a V-shaped valley, hence the name Devil's Dyke.

The historical version features a local man called William Rigden: in the early 19th century, he owned a farm on the site of Hove Park where the stone was located.

At this time, rumours about the Druidic nature of the Goldstone had spread around the country. Together with a rise in the popularity of Druidic-themed literature, this attracted hordes of Victorian sightseers to Rigden's farmland.

To stop the visitors trampling and ruining his crops, Rigden decided to hide the goldstone. He instructed two of his labourers to dig a deep pit, tie the stone in chains and drag it to its new burial place.

It lay hidden here for 35 years until people wondered where it had gone … particularly a man called William Hollamby, who worked for Hove Town Council and was convinced that the Goldstone was a Druidic relic and must be unearthed at once.

After the labourers that originally buried it had been tracked down, the Goldstone was finally unearthed on 29 September 1900. It was erected in its present position in the newly created Hove Park in 1906 and soon began to attract a steady stream of visitors once again.

The Goldstone is alleged to have formed part of an extensive Druid stone circle that once stood in what's now the north-west corner of Hove Park. The rest of the stones are alleged to have been broken up in 1847 and used to fill a pond, remaining hidden for half a century until William Hollamby exhumed them along with the Goldstone. It's alleged that these smaller stones have since been used to form the foundation for the Victoria Fountain. Due to extensive building work and landscaping of the area, historians and archaeologists believe that the original site can no longer be scientifically examined.

Patcham to Rottingdean

1. CHATTRI MEMORIAL — 224
2. PATCHAM PEACE GARDEN — 226
3. DOROTHY STRINGER SCHOOL BUTTERFLY HAVEN — 228
4. PRESTON MANOR — 230
5. BONE GUILLOTINE — 232
6. ROYAL CREST — 234
7. ST PETER'S CHURCH — 236
8. PRESTON WELL HOUSE — 238
9. PRESTON MANOR PET CEMETERY — 240
10. PRESTON MANOR WALLED GARDEN — 242
11. THE "PRESTON TWINS" — 244
12. BOOTH MUSEUM OF NATURAL HISTORY — 246
13. BACKSTAGE AT THE BOOTH MUSEUM OF NATURAL HISTORY — 248
14. THE CASCADE — 250
15. STEVE OVETT'S FOOT — 252
16. K6 PHONE BOXES — 254
17. RICHARD'S GARAGE — 256
18. TAKE SHELTER! MUSEUM — 258
19. REGENCY DRAGONFLIES — 260
20. FLORENCE PLACE JEWISH BURIAL GROUND — 262
21. HOLLINGBURY HILLFORT — 264
22. WILD PARK — 266
23. EARTHSHIP BRIGHTON — 268
24. URBAN FORAGING — 270
25. WOODINGDEAN WELL — 272
26. GLOBALLS JURASSIC MINIATURE GOLF — 274
27. BRIGHTON WALK OF FAME — 276
28. DADDY LONG LEGS REMAINS — 278
29. THE HEAD OF DAVID JACOBS — 280
30. WISHING STONE — 282
31. ST MARGARET'S CHURCH — 283
32. THE KIPLING ROOM — 284
33. BALSDEAN ABANDONED VILLAGE — 286
34. HARVEY'S CROSS — 288

New Road B2112

Beacon Road B2116

Clayton

Underhill Lane

Plumpton

Warningore Wood

Westmeston

Ditchling Road

Highpark Wood

Millbank Wood

23

Stanmer

Great Wood

Falmer

...cham

Carden Avenue

Ditchling Road

24

Falmer

Coldean

Hollingbury

21

22

North Moulsecoomb

...thdean

3

BRIGHTON AND HOVE

Moulsecomb

B2123

5 6 7 & 8

10

Preston

4

Hollingdean

...ulsecoomb

p. 130-161

Bevendean

Warren Road

25

Woodingdean

15

18 20 19

p. 162-197

Bear Road

17

Brighton

Elm Grove

Freshfield Road

Whitehawk

Wilson Avenue

33

041-101

Kemptown

Ovingdean

Greenways

34

Aquarium

H...way

Falmer Road

Rottingdean

p. 021-045

27

26 Roedean 28

29 30 & 31

32

Saltdean

English Channel

0   1 km   2 km

CHATTRI MEMORIAL

A beguiling war memorial to Indian Army soldiers on the South Downs

Standean Lane, Brighton BN1 8ZB
www.chattri.org

Nestled 150 metres above the city of Brighton and Hove on the South Downs, near the area of Patcham, is an unusually beautiful white-domed and pillared memorial. It was built to honour the Indian soldiers who died in the First World War.

From 1914 to 1918, over 1.5 million Indian Army soldiers actively served alongside British troops. Some 12,000 were wounded on the Western Front and hospitalised at sites around Brighton, including the York Place School, the Dome, the Corn Exchange and the Royal Pavilion.

The Chattri memorial was built in recognition of the Indian Army's contribution in helping Allied forces defeat the enemy – particularly the 53 Hindu and Sikh soldiers wounded in battle who died in Brighton after being hospitalised here. The memorial is located on top of the pits in which these soldiers were cremated, before their ashes were scattered in the sea in accordance with their religious rites.

The Chattri, which means "umbrella" in Hindi, Punjabi and Urdu, was designed by architect E.C. Henriques from Mumbai. It symbolises the idea of offering protection to the memory of the dead. Its dome and eight pillars are made out of white Sicilian marble, and the original concrete crematory bases are covered with three large granite slabs.

The monument bears the following inscription in Hindi and English: "To the memory of all the Indian soldiers who gave their lives for their King-Emperor in the Great War, this monument, erected on the site of the funeral pyre where the Hindus and Sikhs who died in hospital at Brighton, passed through the fire, is in grateful admiration and brotherly affection dedicated."

The Prince of Wales unveiled the monument on 21 February 1921.

Another passage to India

India Gate, at the entrance to the Royal Pavilion Gardens, is another memorial commemorating India's relationship with Brighton during the First World War, particularly the role the city's inhabitants played in caring for the wounded Indian soldiers. See p. 86.

A powerful memorial service

Every summer, the Chattri Memorial Group holds a moving remembrance service at the memorial. If you're keen to be part of this event and pay your respects, visit www.chattri.org

PATCHAM PEACE GARDEN

A magical little spot

Old London Road, Patcham BN1 8XN
Open daily from dawn to dusk
Admission free

Just off the main road into Brighton is a tranquil oasis – most Brighton and Hove residents, let alone visitors, haven't a clue it is there.

The century-old Patcham Peace Garden covers an area of around 1.3 hectares of land bought by a prominent local gardener at the time, called Herbert Carden. It was laid out to commemorate those who had served during the First World War.

It's a magical little spot, which seems miles away from the constant whir of traffic on the A23 despite being so close, separated pretty much only by a hedge.

The garden is organised in two halves, the northern half home to a lush grassy area perfect for soaking up the summer sun and enjoying a picnic. The southern half is perhaps the most interesting. It's laid out as a sunken rose garden, complete with a little Doric temple at one end (decorated with fruit motifs and figureheads) and a Tuscan pergola, both of which were bought at the 1924 British Empire Exhibition, held at Wembley.

Today, an active gardening group tends the gardens to maintain them for the enjoyment of the local community … although unfortunately a lot of their work involves picking up the pieces after constant vandalism.

NEARBY
Patcham Court Farm, Vale Avenue, Brighton

A little further north of the Peace Garden, on the north side of Patcham, is one of the borough's oldest farms. The large Grade II-listed farmhouse building, faced in knapped flint, dates from the early 17th century. Extended and considerably restored, it's now a private residence. Although you obviously can't just wander on inside, you might just be able to spot an unusual circular flint building called The Dovecote in the back garden (alongside Church Hill). This scheduled ancient monument, dating back to the 17th century, once used to house nesting doves. Its walls are almost 1 metre thick and it contains 550 nesting boxes. It's also said to retain the original swinging ladder, which would have been used to reach all the nesting boxes, and is the only one of its kind in the city. When in full production, it would have produced up to 200 young featherless birds (or squabs) a week for the table.

DOROTHY STRINGER SCHOOL BUTTERFLY HAVEN

A giant hidden butterfly hotel

Dorothy Stringer School, Stringer Way, Brighton BN1 6QG
Access is by public footpath through the school grounds: open daily
Admission free

Populations of urban butterflies are in dramatic decline for various reasons. However, Brighton and Hove is one UK city that has been particularly successful in luring them back by establishing what are known as "butterfly havens" – chalky beds of wildflowers – hidden in various parks and green spaces around the city.

These havens are the unique design of Brighton resident, teacher and multi-award-winning bioeducationalist Dr Dan Danahar – known affectionately around town as "the Butterfly Man". He created the first haven in 2007 in the grounds of Dorothy Stringer High School (where he teaches) by exposing the chalk beneath the playing fields and getting pupils to plant 40,000 wild flowers. Everyone is welcome to visit it.

"The idea behind the havens is to maintain high biodiversity and create a microclimate that supports various species – a surrogate habitat, if you like, which we've done by manipulating the microclimate using the typography," says Dan.

Half the size of a football pitch, the Dorothy Stringer butterfly haven has hosted 29 different butterflies (out of a total of 59 known species in the UK) since it was created. It has even attracted Britain's tiniest butterfly, the small blue, which is rare and previously thought not particularly adept at navigating cities. "We've got unbelievable numbers of common butterflies such as the common blue and small blue all over the site now," adds Dan.

His award-winning design is based on years of research (including a doctorate) on bioengineering and microclimates. This has since been rolled out in 25 parks and green spaces around the city in collaboration with Brighton & Hove City Council.

"It doesn't cost a council much to create these havens," says Dan. "All they need is someone with a bulldozer to scrape the turf off the chalk before some local wild flower plugs are put in, which kids love doing, turning it into a whole community-wide engagement."

Other butterfly sanctuaries around Brighton

The largest butterfly haven in Brighton and Hove is located in East Brighton Park, where volunteers helped plant 10,000 wild flowers in 2014. Other locations include Woodingdean Park, Hove Park, Hollingbury Park and Brighthelm Gardens, to name but a few, with others in the pipeline.

PRESTON MANOR

A mysterious historic home

Preston Drove, Brighton BN1 6SD
Tel: 0300 029 0900
http://brightonmuseums.org.uk/prestonmanor/
Open: 1 April–30 Sept, Tues–Sat 10am–5pm, Sun 2pm–5pm

With its secluded location surrounded by trees, most people walk past Preston Manor without realising it's there. Those who *have* heard of it don't know much about what it's used for or what's inside.

"We've been a museum for 84 years, but many locals still seem unaware of the house or, if they have heard of it, have no idea of its function," says Paula Wrightson, the Museum Learning Officer. "People coming here by taxi have been dropped off at all sorts of weird places – once in the middle of Preston Park!"

Once you've found the manor house, wander up the gravel drive and in through the big front door: you'll discover a magnificent historic home that paints an evocative picture of Edwardian and post-Edwardian life, both upstairs and downstairs.

The property originates from the 13th century, but the house we see today dates from the 18th and 20th centuries. It was decorated by the Stanford family, who owned it for over 200 years, starting with William – at his death in 1841, he was thought to be the richest private individual in

Sussex. Heirs Sir Charles and Lady Ellen Thomas-Stanford restored the house to the glory of its Edwardian heyday, furnishing it with many pieces from the 17th, 18th and 19th centuries. After their death, it was opened to the public in 1933 as the Thomas Stanford Museum.

The collections on show include ceramics, glass, silver and clocks. The guided tour takes in the servants' quarters and hall, butlers' pantry, boot hall, kitchen, head housemaids' and personal maids' rooms, together with a period walled garden and a graveyard for family pets (see pp. 240 and 242).

The most haunted house in Britain?

Once discovered, what's perhaps most surprising about Preston Manor is that it's said to be the most haunted house in Britain. For many years, it was supposedly haunted by a blonde woman dressed in white – several guests complained of unexplained happenings! According to Rose Collis in *The New Encyclopaedia of Brighton*, Living TV's *Most Haunted* team filmed a programme on Preston Manor in 1996: they claimed they had experienced one of their most active nights of paranormal activity.

BONE GUILLOTINE

A macabre ornament

Preston Manor, Preston Drove, Brighton BN1 6SD
Tel: 0300 029 0900
http://brightonmuseums.org.uk/prestonmanor/
Open: 1 April–30 Sept, Tues–Sat 10am–5pm, Sun 2pm–5pm

Hiding among all the chintzy fine china, antiques and oil paintings at Preston Manor (see p 230) is a delicately crafted oddity with a gruesome history.

Upstairs on the landing, inside a small glass box on the shelf of a dark-wood cabinet, is an intricate model of a guillotine. It was made out of bone by French prisoners of war held at Lewes Castle in around 1800.

Donated in 1936 by the wife of a local collector, Mrs Mary Clelan Somers Clarke, it tells the story of a turbulent time in Europe's history around 1790, when the Napoleonic Wars were raging in France.

"A huge number of prisoners of war were brought over to England from France at this time and held in Lewes Castle just seven miles from here," says Paula Wrightson, Museum Learning Officer at Preston Manor. "Many of them weren't necessarily career soldiers, but artisans and makers by trade. If you look at the intricacy of this model, it shows the considerable skill involved in making it."

Markets used to be held in the castle prison. Here prisoners would sell objects they made out of wood and bone to people in the area who came to look at them. 'This was one of these objects," says Paula. "And the prisoners wouldn't have made it due to a gruesome mindset, they would have chosen it as they knew it would sell, as it was what people were talking about at the time."

On a closer look, you can see that the guillotine is a working model, complete with a rope that moves the blade up and down.

According to Paula, "The guillotine was based on a collaborative design between Dr Antoine Louis and Dr Joseph-Ignace Guillotin for the governing body of France, who commissioned them to come up with a 'humanitarian' method of doing away with unwanted members of society. Although throughout its use, it was always deemed controversial."

You'll find a more elaborate version of this guillotine in the Willet Gallery at Brighton Museum.

One of the owners of Preston Manor, Charles Thomas-Stanford, bought Lewes Castle in 1922 and donated it to the Sussex Archaeological Society, now Sussex Past.

ROYAL CREST

*A spurious decoration on Brighton's
hidden manor house*

Preston Manor, Preston Drove, Brighton BN1 6SD
Tel: 0300 029 0900
http://brightonmuseums.org.uk/prestonmanor/
Open: 1 April–30 Sept: Tues–Sat 10am–5pm, Sun 2pm–5pm
Admission free

Even if you've discovered Preston Manor (see p. 230), it's unlikely you'll have spotted a hidden Tudor-style royal crest lurking at the back of the building on the remains of an old tower.

"Early to mid-20th century photographs of the south side of Preston Manor show the house covered in greenery, probably Virginia creeper – the leaves go bright red in the autumn," says Paula Wrightson, Museum Learning Officer at the manor. "In some old photographs, the crest is grown over by ivy but in others the greenery has been clipped back to keep the crest visible. Still, most people only know about it if it's pointed out to them."

In the late 1800s, the manor's owner, Eleanor MacDonald, added a beautiful Tudor-style tower to this south side of the building, to house a toilet and smoking room; the stone royal crest was added on the outside.

"Preston Manor in an early form was here in the Tudor period, but not as a royal house," says Paula, "although the family at the time liked to make links with its Tudor heritage.

"They also believed it was one of the houses given to Anne of Cleves after the settlement following her marriage annulment from Henry VIII, although it was later discovered this wasn't true. The crest still remains, nevertheless."

No one knows for sure who designed or made the crest. According to Paula, "It's likely to have come from a commercial supplier of these kinds of decorative pieces, just as we buy stone ornaments and plaques for our gardens today."

When Mrs MacDonald died and her daughter Ellen, along with her husband Charles Thomas-Stanford, moved in, they had the house remodelled and the tower removed. However, they were careful to keep the crest, as well as another crest found next to it.

"This second crest is said to belong to the Benett-Stanford family – referring to Ellen's first husband, Vere Fane-Benett – combined with the Stanford arms," explains Paula. "Ellen and Vere married in 1867 and Vere died in 1894 – by this time, the crest would have been in position next to the royal crest."

Another architectural Tudor-style feature – a Tudor Rose – saved from the tower can be seen on the front lawn used as a birdbath.

ST PETER'S CHURCH

Brighton's oldest building

Preston Park, Preston Road, Brighton BN1 6SD
Tel: 01273 553249
www.stpetersprestonpark.co.uk
Open daily 10.30am–3.30pm; longer in the summer
Admission free

Built in 1250, when the area of Preston was just a small village, the Grade II-listed St Peter's Church is considered to be the oldest building in Brighton.

Design-wise, this simple and compact structure consists of a nave, chancel and tower. Until 1872, it was filled with tall-box pews for rent and backless benches for the poor. In the early 20th century, a new larger church – St John's – was built nearby to accommodate Brighton's growing congregation. In 1990 St Peter's passed into the care of the Churches Conservation Trust, which now opens it to the public.

Inside, it's a treasure trove of artefacts offering clues to the town's interesting past, many found in the tiny chancel. The altar is considered unusual in that it was originally the chest tomb of a man called Edward Elrington, who lived in Preston Manor around 1500. Meanwhile, wall plaques and stained-glass windows commemorate the manor's later owners, the Thomas-Stanford and MacDonald families.

On two of the window recesses, Edwardian stencilling shows the "crossed keys", the symbol of St Peter, who, according to the Bible, holds the keys to heaven. A set of beautiful oak pews boasts stunning detailed carvings, showing the head of an American Indian, a monk, kings and queens and a pelican feeding her baby birds in their nest.

However, perhaps the most notable artefacts are three remaining 13th-century wall paintings from a collection that once covered the entire wall above and around the chancel arch. They were whitewashed over during the Reformation in the 16th century, rediscovered in 1830 and then damaged by fire in 1906. These three paintings survive, albeit faintly, and depict the Nativity, St Michael weighing souls, and the murder of Thomas Becket by the Knights of King Henry II in Canterbury Cathedral in 1170.

The murder of Isaac Gold

Inside the church, to the right of the entrance, is a wall plaque commemorating a Mr Isaac Gold. He was an investment banker who lived in Preston Park and regularly travelled to London for business. On 27 June 1881, he was brutally murdered on the London to Brighton train by fellow passenger Percy Lefroy Mapleton, who became the first person to be caught using photofit technology printed on a "Wanted" poster.

PRESTON WELL HOUSE

The "lost" well of Preston Village

Preston Croquet Club grounds, Preston Drove, Brighton BN1 6LA
Open when the croquet club is open (Mon, Wed and Sat mornings from
9.45am) or through the fence from the grounds of St Peter's Church (see p. 236)
Admission free

Tucked at the side of St Peter's Church inside the grounds of the Preston Park Croquet Club is an intriguing little curio. It doesn't look like much at first glance; however, this clump of overgrowth is actually the ruins of an 18th-century, Grade II-listed knapped flint well house. What's even more fascinating is that it was built to cover an 18-metre well dating back to 1552 – which still exists.

"The well was once used to gather water from Brighton's 'lost' river, the Wellesbourne, which runs under Preston Village and down to the area known as Pool Valley near the seafront – hence its name," says Paula Wrightson, Museum Learning Officer at Preston Manor.

"It was at one time the only water supply for Preston Village. When Preston Manor (see p. 230) was rebuilt in 1738, a primitive engine with a vertical shaft, turned by a horse driving a 'gin' (a beam or yoke) in a circle, was put up over the well to supply water for the manor," she adds.

Although today it's mostly overgrown with brambles, you can just about make out the two arched doorways facing west, three arched doorways facing north, and a doorway plus a small window to the east. It's not known why these doorways have been bricked up, "perhaps to make them stronger", says Paula. "What's also interesting is that the upper part once housed a pigeon house."

The Stanmer Park well house

There's a restored version of this type of well house at Stanmer House in Stanmer Park, in the church grounds. It was rebuilt in 1838, when the new Stanmer Church was commissioned by the landowner, the third Earl of Chichester, Henry Thomas Pelham. His family had begun their association with the village in the 16th century and took ownership of the whole estate and its lands in the early 18th century. The nearby Grade I-listed Stanmer House was built in 1722. The Pelhams then demolished the original houses and buildings of the old village and created the estate-village we see today.

PRESTON MANOR
PET CEMETERY

A bizarre hidden burial ground

Inside Preston Manor walled garden
Preston Park, Preston Road, Brighton BN1 6SD
Open: April–Sept 10am–6pm, Oct–March 10am–4pm
Admission free

Tucked away in the north corner of Preston Manor's beautiful walled garden – a hidden gem in itself (see p. 242) – are a few tiny mildewed gravestones that stand testament to the Victorian tradition of burying beloved pets in special cemeteries.

This particular pet cemetery was founded by Mrs Eleanor MacDonald and her twin daughters, Lily and Diana, who lived at Preston Manor in the late 19th century.

Today there are 16 dogs and three cats buried here, including dogs belonging to Preston Manor's most well-known owner, Lady Ellen Thomas-Stanford.

The miniature gravestones bear epitaphs you can just about make out. They range from the touching to the macabre, most offering personal tributes: "In memory of Dear Soot who for nine years was our faithful friend and playfellow who was cruelly poisoned. Died in consequence July 17th 1884"; "In memory of dear Peter who was crossy and sulky but died December 1886"; "Peter was a Scotch terrier and he bit everyone in a white apron".

Remembering George The Pavilion Cat

The gravestone that people find most intriguing is inscribed "George the Pavilion Cat" a shorthaired black and white cat who lived at the Royal Pavilion from 1965 to 1980. Historic houses always kept cats to catch vermin and the Royal Pavilion was no different: Preston Manor (see p. 230) kept a cat for this reason as recently as the 1990s. *George the Pavilion Cat*, a charming illustrated book written by Judy Pennington, tells the story of George. It is for sale at Preston Manor and the Royal Pavilion.

London's hidden pet cemetery

Another famous pet cemetery lies tucked behind the Victoria Gate Lodge in Hyde Park, one of the hidden gems of London (see *Secret London: an unusual guide* by Rachel Howard and Bill Nash, from the same publisher). To visit this cemetery, you must book at least one month in advance with the Royal Parks. Founded in 1880 and now largely hidden behind thick undergrowth, Hyde Park's pet cemetery is home to over 300 deceased pets, including dogs, cats, birds and even a monkey.

PRESTON MANOR
WALLED GARDEN

A secret historic kitchen garden

Preston Park, Preston Road, Brighton BN1 6SD
Open: April–Sept 10am–6pm, Oct–March 10am–4pm
Admission free

For centuries, most large country houses had a walled kitchen garden. They were highly productive places, supplying food, herbs and flowers for the family, staff and guests of the big house.

You'll find a stunning example of an Edwardian kitchen garden lurking behind Preston Manor (see p. 230); it was restored in 2000 with £750,000 of National Lottery funding. Today, it's run and maintained by Brighton & Hove City Council and an army of passionate volunteers, and is open for the public to enjoy.

Originally laid out in 1905, it is what's called an old-fashioned "Queen Anne" garden, divided into four plots, the whole forming a square with a sundial in the middle – although the sundial has had to be removed due to persistent vandalism. There's also a beautiful arched gateway, rebuilt in 1983, and a lovely formal lily pond – the original lost when the road was widened in 1972.

The beds are packed with traditional cottage garden favourites such as dahlias, poppies, delphiniums, and older-variety scented and rambling roses. There are also structural plants like pampas grass and scented shrubs such as lilac. The garden has an unusual and very large mulberry tree and a laburnum arch beloved of the Edwardians – this looks absolutely beautiful when it blooms around late April or early to mid-May.

Although the layout we see today is considered Edwardian or Victorian, a plan from 1617 shows that an established walled garden already existed in this location.

The walled garden was recently used as the setting for the first-ever hand-fasting ceremony – essentially a pagan wedding. It took place on the Winter Solstice (21 December) in 2016.

A miniature burial ground

In the south-west corner of the garden, you'll spot a row of miniature headstones lining the back walls. This hidden gem is known as the Preston Manor pet cemetery (see p. 240). In the late Victorian and Edwardian eras, pets were considered important family members in wealthy homes. When they died, they were buried in private cemeteries complete with headstones and heartfelt inscriptions.

THE "PRESTON TWINS"

The oldest English elm trees in Europe

Coronation Garden, Preston Park, Preston Road, Brighton BN1 6SD

Brighton and Hove is home to more types of elm tree than any other city in the world. It was granted National Collection Status in 1998 due to its groundbreaking work protecting the city's trees from Dutch elm disease, which ravaged the UK elm population in the 1970s, killing more than 60 million trees.

As a result of this work, the city's population of elms has doubled in the past 30 to 40 years. Preston Park is considered a living museum as it's home to around 30 different types, including the "Preston Twins", thought to be the oldest English elms in Europe – and possibly the world.

These hollow giants – you can actually stand inside one of them – are estimated to be some 400 years old and have a girth of about 6 metres. They're believed to be the last of the ancient elm trees, which originally formed a hedgerow in the area – long gone from the local landscape.

Elm trees were originally brought to Brighton and Hove by the Victorians and Edwardians, who planted them in their thousands in field hedgerows all around the area. They were also widely used to make furniture, coffins, and wheel hubs for carts and wagons, and often featured in the paintings of Turner and Constable (see p. 50).

Elm trees are one of the few species of larger tree that thrives in the area's chalky alkaline soil and salty atmosphere. They are a boon to the city, providing cleaner air and wildlife habitation.

The Preston Twins are home to a colony of rare White-letter Hairstreak butterflies, which exclusively live on elm trees.

How to spot an elm

Elms have asymmetrical leaves with one long and one short lobe. They flower early in the year and have purple blossom in March.

To help visitors discover the city's elm collection, two students from Brighton University, together with various local organisations and associations, have created a "Brighton and Hove Elm Tree Trail" map – this shows the location of some of the best clusters of elm trees in the city. There's also a children's version of the map, which includes fun facts, word searches and activities. You can download them both at www.brightonelmtrees.com

If you look closely at one of the Preston Twins, with a little imagination, you might see the shape of a dragon's head sticking out of the trunk.

BOOTH MUSEUM OF NATURAL HISTORY

One of Brighton's most off-the-beaten-path museums

194 Dyke Rd, Brighton BN1 5AA
Tel: 0300 029 0900
www.brightonmuseums.org.uk/booth
Open: Mon–Wed, Fri and Sat 10am–12pm, 1.15pm–5pm
Admission free

For a cultural establishment with groundbreaking credentials, the Booth Museum's location and premises are remarkably ordinary. Looks can be deceptive, though, for inside this giant plain red-brick building, set back on a road out of Brighton, is what's been described worldwide as "the original home of the diorama".

Founded in 1874, the Booth Museum of Natural History was the first of its kind to display taxidermy birds in their natural habitat. It's an idea since copied all over the world and perfected by the likes of New York's American Museum of Natural History and the Smithsonian Institution in Washington, no less.

Inside you'll find a vast gallery resembling a Victorian attic belonging to a compulsive collector, complete with a musty, lingering smell. It's a truly spectacular collection of 300 dioramas lined up along the walls and showing every British bird, stuffed and in its natural habitat, from seagulls and owls to hawks and starlings.

The museum was created by Edward Thomas Booth, a typical affluent Victorian, who was exposed to shooting, the natural world and taxidermy at an early age. He eventually developed a serious ambition – to exhibit an example of every species of British bird.

Once he'd achieved his goal, Booth started collecting species from all around the world, from birds of paradise to parrots – even returning with the skeleton of a Dodo, that mysterious and beautiful extinct flightless bird found on the island of Mauritius until the 17th century. Not to mention 525,000 insects, 50,000 minerals and rocks, 30,000 plants and 5,000 microscope slides, old specimens such as shells from the bottom of a 55-million-year-old Mediterranean lagoon and dinosaur bones.

By 1874, Booth's collection of birds and taxidermy had outgrown his marital home, Bleak House on Dyke Road, so he built a new setting for it in his garden – the Booth Museum building we know today.

The Booth Museum runs exclusive, behind-the-scenes private group tours, offering the chance to see the hidden collections in its stores and hear more about the history of this quirky local treasure (see p. 248).

BACKSTAGE AT THE BOOTH MUSEUM OF NATURAL HISTORY

Secret collections …

194 Dyke Rd, Brighton BN1 5AA
Tel: 0300 029 0900
https://brightonmuseums.org.uk/booth/plan-your-visit/
behind-the-scenes-tours/
Tours can be booked in advance all year round (min. groups of 5, max. 15): call
Brighton Museums' visitor services on the number above

A s Brighton's most eccentric and off-the-beaten-track museum, the Booth is a hidden gem in itself (see p. 246). However, it's also the setting for one of the city's most intriguing tours.

"Backstage at the Booth" offers curious visitors the opportunity to go behind the "Staff only" signs to discover the museum's secret stores. They are home to just under 1 million objects relating to the natural world – the basis of an extensive research collection.

"We regularly host scientists from around the world who use our collections for research," says curator Lee Ismail. "Recently they've come from as far as Russia, Alberta in Canada and Florida. We've even had a team from Stanford and Manchester universities borrow our type specimen fossil of the earliest known flowering plant – they CT-scanned it and studied it virtually, using the equipment at Stanford University in California."

Tours of this vast backstage anthology take place during the day, and occasionally in the evening, and last around 2 hours. They start in the lower gallery and move up into the stores above the galleries, which you can look down on.

It's a fascinating, all-consuming experience as you walk up and down creaky corridors, past wooden cases of dusty drawers filled with butterflies and bugs, bones, eggs and shells, and cupboards filled with fossils, minerals and rocks – not to mention the 9,000 mounted birds and other creatures you can spot hidden away. Your journey throughout is peppered with anecdotes about the museum's eccentric affluent founder, Edward Thomas Booth, and fascinating stories of the natural world.

"I like showing people our pangolin," says Lee, who takes the tours, pointing out some of the most intriguing objects in the collection. "It's one of my favourite things here, not only because I love them, but also to highlight their important tragic story as the world's most trafficked animals. They are killed in their millions for medical treatments that do not work – their blood and scales are the same as our blood and fingernails."

"We have a fossil fish that is around 65 million years old and a coco de mer, the largest seed in the world. We also hold the most extensive collection of lepidoptera butterflies outside the national collection and the largest collection of bird breastbones in the world," he adds. "People are so surprised when they discover what's behind the scenes at the Booth Museum, as most have no idea of the scale of our collections."

THE CASCADE

Brighton's only waterfall

The Rockery, London Road, Brighton BN1
Admission free
Bus 5 bus stops just outside

Frequently overlooked in favour of Preston Park is an award-winning garden called The Rockery, which happens to be the setting for Brighton's one and only waterfall. This rock garden – considered the biggest in Britain – is set on the side of an old railway bank across the main road from Preston Park. This was once a wooded area called The Rookery, bought at the same time as land used to create the park.

The garden, complete with its secret 30-metre-high water feature, was designed in 1935 by Captain B. MacLaren, Brighton's superintendent of parks. He landscaped it using 1.3 tonnes of rocks bought from a quarry in the West Country for £4,000. They were transported into the new park on a railway line specially laid at the top of the garden, to allow them to be tipped out into place easily.

"It was a huge expense at the time and incredible to think about it now," says Sue Shepherd, chair of the Friends of Preston Park. "Men had to do their best with poles to guide the rocks down the hill to where they had to go. While they were doing it, a man stood in the road with a flag, ready to alert drivers should any of the rocks tumble down the bank onto the A23, putting drivers at risk!"

The garden is designed to be interesting all year round and is looked after by one main gardener, Andy Jeavons, and an army of volunteers. Although it's just under 1 hectare in size, it feels so much bigger: a wander around its winding stone pathways is a magical experience, particularly in spring, when the 400 tree whips and 25,000 English bluebells – a haven for insects and birds – burst into bloom.

Around each corner there's a new area to discover, whether it's a small patch of secluded grass or a bench hidden in the trees, the pond with its little bridge, the giant stepping stones, the stunning views over Brighton or the old summer house built to MacLaren's design. Once a café serving hot drinks, it's now used to store garden equipment.

STEVE OVETT'S FOOT

The remnants of Brighton's sporting hero

Preston Park, Brighton BN1

Next to the Preston Park rose garden is a sculpture of a foot on a plinth, or rather the remains of a bronze statue of Brighton-born athlete, Steve Ovett. As a world-record holder at 1,500 metres and a mile, and gold-medal winner in the 800 metres at the 1980 Moscow Games – a moment rated one of the most iconic in the history of the Olympics – Ovett has become known as one of the world's greatest athletes, a "national treasure" and Brighton's best sporting hero.

The bronze statue, designed by local artist and sculptor Pete Webster, took four years to make. It was unveiled in 1987 to commemorate Ovett's achievements and phenomenal success. However, in 2007, it was cut down and stolen – the thieves taking all but the left foot, which still remains in Preston Park.

A new statue made out of the remaining pieces from the original – only the leg was found – was unveiled on the first day of the London 2012 Olympics, this time on Brighton seafront. Again, it was designed by Pete Webster, who worked with researchers in 3D technology at the University of Brighton to help create the new design.

The statue was strategically placed at a point that marks 800 metres and back again from the Brighton Palace Pier, a nod to Ovett's 1980 triumph in Moscow.

Steve Ovett's achievements are marked by a plaque in the Brighton Walk of Fame at Brighton Marina (see p. 276).

Pete Webster also created the statue of Brighton-born variety performer Max Miller, which you'll spot hidden in the flowerbeds at the entrance to the Pavilion Gardens on New Road (see p. 74).

K6 PHONE BOXES

16

Brighton's miniature listed buildings

Powis Square, Brighton

On the edge of Powis Square, in the fashionable Cliftonville area of Brighton, sits an example of a British design classic: two K6 telephone boxes, rendered obsolete by the mobile phone!

They were designed in 1935 by Sir Giles Gilbert Scott to commemorate the Silver Jubilee of King George V and – strange as it might seem to us now – were initially widely reviled. Scott won a General Post Office competition to design a phone box to replace the first-ever 1921 model. All the prototypes were put into service around London, but Scott's winning design is the only one that survives.

The K6 – which stands for Kiosk 6 – was the first red phone box to be used extensively outside of London and many thousands were installed in virtually every town and city. It's thought around 60,000 of these K6 kiosks were installed nationwide, although vandalism and high maintenance costs unfortunately led to them being gradually withdrawn and replaced by utilitarian modern booths. By December 2013, there were only 10,762 examples remaining, of which only 2,562 were listed.

At one time, there was an active scheme to convert the old kiosks into mobile phone masts. After a conservation campaign in the 1990s, some of the old phone boxes have been renovated and reinstalled. The rest have been sold off for scrap or as souvenirs. Despite their demise, they have become an instantly recognisable icon of 20th-century Britain.

As well as these two at Powis Square, you'll find several other listed tomato-red phone boxes around Brighton and Hove – in Bedford Square, Marine Parade, Dyke Road, New Road, St Peter's Place and Upper North Street, to name but a few.

From designing phone boxes to power stations

Sir Giles Gilbert Scott was also the architect of Brighton College and the now-demolished Brill Baths, which used to be in East Street. He designed many London icons, including Waterloo Bridge, Battersea Power Station and Bankside Power Station – now the Tate Modern.

17

RICHARD'S GARAGE

Brighton's earliest known petrol pumps

19a Bath Street, Brighton BN1 3TB

I f there's one house that stands out among the rows of whitewashed Victorian terraces on Bath Street in Seven Dials, it's number 19a, with its two striking, well-preserved Shellmex petrol pumps dating back to the 1950s or 1960s.

Unfortunately, records on the house's history are patchy and hard to come by. However it's thought that it was originally the home of Richard's Garage, a mini petrol station and mechanic's yard opened around 1962 by a local man called Richard Busse – although some say the business was established much earlier, in 1885. Busse is said to have died in 2011 and the pumps served petrol until 2010. The building was subsequently renovated and turned into a private home.

Today, the pumps have been painted blue, although they were brown when the garage was in operation, along with the rest of the garage front.

Local listing

In 2013 the Shellmex petrol pumps were included in a draft list of historically important landmarks put forward by Brighton and Hove residents for "local listing". A Locally Listed Heritage Asset is a building, park or garden considered to be of special interest because of its local historic, architectural, design or townscape value and is designated at a local level by the council, but it isn't the same as a listed building designated by Historic England. The local list is reviewed every five years. Other locally listed landmarks around Brighton and Hove include the 19th-century cast-iron bollards near the entrance to St Nicholas's Church on Dyke Road, London Road railway station building in Shaftesbury Place, Preston Circus fire station and Hove Town Hall.

TAKE SHELTER! MUSEUM

A secret underground war museum

Downs Junior School, Rugby Road, Brighton BN1 6ED
www.takeshelter.org.uk
Open for guided tours and special events throughout the Brighton Fringe Festival

A school isn't the most obvious location for a war museum, let alone underneath the school. However, if you venture beneath Downs Junior School in the Fiveways area of Brighton, you'll find just that – an amazing underground museum hidden beneath the playground in a series of tunnels that once served as an air raid shelter.

The shelter is the largest of three built under the school's playgrounds in 1939 – it's the only one currently accessible. "The Trenches", as it was referred to at the time, according to an old log book, is made from pre-cast concrete panels and lies approximately 3 metres below the playground. In an air raid, it could accommodate 300 children on bench seating along each corridor – the shelter was also used by the local community during night-time raids.

After the Second World War, the two main staircase entrances were removed and sealed. The shelter remained hidden for over 30 years, until a workman hired to clean the drains stumbled on it in 1985.

In 2012 a small group of volunteers from the Friends of Downs Junior School, led by the school premises manager, Michael Button, had the idea of turning the tunnels into a museum. The project has taken about five years to get to the stage it's at today, relying on funding and donations from local businesses, and the hard work of volunteers. It has since been recognised by the Brighton & Hove Heritage Learning Partnership.

The result is a wonderful immersive museum experience aimed at school groups – although it's fascinating for all – which you can visit on a 45-minute guided tour. Exhibits, video, sound and other interactive features are used to tell the story of the Second World War – particularly Brighton's part in it – and explore the themes of evacuation, blackout, rationing, the Blitz, D-Day and VE Day.

Special features include recreations of a 1940s kitchen and bedroom, the chance to experience what an air raid and bombing would have felt like if you were in the tunnels, as well as extracts from *Sheltered Lives*, a fascinating book published by the school in 1994 that documents stories of ex-pupils who used the shelter during the war.

The team behind Take Shelter! have recently organised a reprint of *Sheltered Lives*. It is available to buy from their website: www.takeshelter.org.uk

REGENCY DRAGONFLIES

Recycled art

Veolia Materials Recovery Facility, Hollingdean Lane, Brighton BN1 7BB

This gigantic purpose-built recycling plant is largely unexceptional – a tall, futuristic building clad in metal with a few windows for daylight. However, local artists Lucy Williams, Chris Hawkins and Amy Douglas have managed to add interest to it and turn it into something of a landmark in Hollingdean – one of the least lovely parts of Brighton and Hove – by decorating the front of the building with three giant illuminated dragonflies.

In keeping with the theme of reusing and recycling, these three over-sized insects known as the Regency Dragonflies are made entirely of recycled materials, all collected locally. The intricate wing patterns are made of an aluminium composite – a lightweight and ecologically sound material – and echo the exotic Regency designs in the world-famous Royal Pavilion.

They also light up, using ever-changing LED lights. This gives the impression that the dragonflies are hovering over the building and represents the delicate balance of our ecosystem. The idea is that the dragonflies will help to educate local schoolchildren, who visit the facility on a weekly basis, about the importance of sustainable development and recycling.

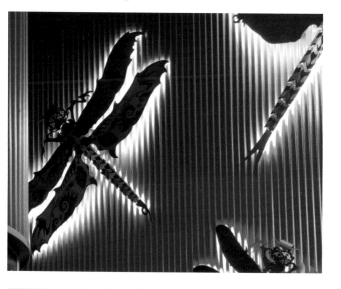

Lucy Williams, one of the artists behind the Regency Dragonflies, also designed the brightly coloured signs that grace both entrances to Brighton's Open Market near The Level.

FLORENCE PLACE JEWISH BURIAL GROUND

Brighton's oldest Jewish cemetery

Florence Place, Brighton BN1
Tel: 01273 888855
www.bhhc-shul.org/contact.html
Contact the Brighton & Hove Hebrew Congregation office
(at the above phone no.) for information about visits and/or appointments
Admission free

Permanently locked gates and a neglected, overgrown appearance suggest that the Florence Place Jewish burial ground is derelict. It's not.

This curious cemetery, which belongs to the Brighton & Hove Hebrew Congregation, is in fact fully operational. This is where some of the city's most notable Jews are buried. It's also considered a rare example of a minority faith burial ground of its time.

"There are about 30 graves still to be filled and the cemetery remains a cemetery until 100 years after the last grave is filled, so there is no risk of demolition," says David Seidel of the Brighton & Hove Hebrew Congregation.

According to a plaque on a wall to the left of the gates, it was built on land given to the Brighton Synagogue congregation by Thomas Read Kemp, one of the major developers of modern Brighton, in 1826.

The cemetery opens occasionally for events or private tours, but if you're just passing, a little peek through the gates reveals a striking red-brick octagonal mortuary chapel – now Grade II-listed – which was designed by local architect Thomas Lainson. You'll also see a big white ceramic sink on the side of the building, a feature in keeping with the Jewish tradition for people to wash their hands as they leave the "presence of death".

Among the Brighton Jewish community's notable figures laid to rest here are Henry Soloman, Chief Constable of Brighton (see p. 80); Hyam Lewis, a Brighton town commissioner; Sir John Howard, philanthropist and engineer; and Levi Emanuel Cohen, founder and editor of the *Brighton Guardian*.

NEARBY
A landmarked tram shelter

Other nearby sights include an early 20th-century tram shelter on Ditchling Road – although it has seen better days, it's been designated a local landmark.

Home to a holocaust memorial

Most burials among Brighton's Jewish community took place at Florence Place until the bigger Meadow View Jewish cemetery, just off Bear Lane, was built in 1919. Meadow View is notable for its airy location on top of the Downs and has a large burial chamber with a prayer hall. There's also a moving Holocaust Memorial sculpture in the grounds.

HOLLINGBURY HILLFORT

An ancient sight in suburbia

Hollingbury Park golf course, Ditchling Road, Brighton BN1

With its unattractive industrial estate, it's unlikely that Hollingbury features in many – if any – guidebooks. However, venture uphill out of central Brighton to this suburban area and you'll find one of Brighton and Hove's oldest sights.

Just off Ditchling Road, take the path through Hollingbury Park golf course to the western edge of Wild Park (see p. 266), where you'll spot a large raised mound of earth covered in shrubs. This is what's known as Hollingbury Hillfort, or Hollingbury Castle, a remarkable Iron Age fort over 2,000 years old. The site evolved over a long period – from the 6th century to about the middle of the 2nd century bc. It has seen use as a Bronze Age burial ground, an Iron Age fortification and, later, a Romano-British settlement.

Although it's commonly referred to as a castle, it certainly never was one. The site was excavated by Herbert Toms in 1908, Cecil Curwen and the Brighton and Hove Archaeological Society in 1931, and John Holmes in 1967, according to Rose Collis in *The New Encyclopaedia of Brighton*. The excavations uncovered ramparts once defended by wooden barricades and the sites of wooden huts, offering a valuable insight into prehistoric life.

As well as a window into Brighton's Iron Age past, the Hillfort is one of the best places for a view over the surrounding area. These hills lying to the north of Brighton, between London Road and Lewes Road valleys, reach 180 metres above sea level and offer the widest panorama in the city. On a clear day, you'll be able to see to the New Forest, the Isle of Wight, Chanctonbury Ring (another hill fort), the North Downs, Hastings and, of course, across Brighton and Hove.

Hill forts around Sussex

There are several hill forts dotted around Sussex, the largest of which is Cissbury Ring in Worthing, about 5 km from the town centre. It's dubbed "one of the jewels in the crown" of the South Downs National Park and described by the National Trust as the most historic hill in the park. It's the second largest hill fort in England, and one of the largest in Britain and Europe overall, covering some 60 acres (24 hectares). It's an excellent habitat for butterflies, flowers and rare plants. The earthworks that form the fortifications were built around the beginning of the Middle Iron Age, possibly around 250 bc, but were abandoned in the period between 50 bc and ad 50.

WILD PARK

An overlooked city nature reserve

South Downs National Park, Lewes Road, Brighton BN1 9JS
Buses 23, 24 and 25 go past the park every few minutes during the day.
There's a pay car park.

Brighton and Hove residents – and visitors – are spoiled for choice when it comes to getting out into nature, the city packed with popular parks and surrounded by glorious countryside. However, few often don't realise that the beauty of the South Downs National Park can be experienced without actually leaving the city.

You'll find Wild Park just 10 minutes from the centre of Brighton, just off the busy main road that runs through the suburb of Moulsecoomb. Despite its unremarkable location, this little-known green space officially forms part of the South Downs National Park – and at 90 acres, is one of the largest local nature reserves in the city.

What's also fascinating about it is that when Brighton & Hove City Council – then known as the Brighton Corporation – bought the park in 1925, there were no trees growing in it. Today, it's unrecognisable having been left to return to its original wild state. It offers everything a rambler would expect to find on a walk through this typical undulating Sussex countryside, including birds and butterflies to spot, woodland trails to follow, wildflower beds, a 17th-century dew pond and some burial mounds.

Those up for a hiking challenge might like to find the hill known as the "ski slope". This takes you up to the ancient Hollingbury Hillfort (see p. 264) and offers some of the best views over the surrounding South Downs, across the city rooftops of Brighton and Hove, all the way down to the sea.

Wild Park's grazing sheep

All around Wild Park, you might notice signs alerting walkers to grazing sheep. Brighton & Hove City Council uses flocks of sheep at various sights around Brighton to help maintain and restore the natural diversity of the ancient flower-rich grasslands. Grazing is thought to protect the landscape better than mechanical mowing for various reasons. For example, it allows insects – which would usually get caught in the blades – time to move out of the way, and ensures structures like anthills aren't damaged. It also helps to keep aggressive weeds under control and makes sure brambles don't take over: this encourages more wildflowers to grow, attracting insects such as butterflies and bees. Seven New Forest ponies have recently joined the sheep to graze the city grassland, all of them looked after by a group of specially trained volunteers.

EARTHSHIP BRIGHTON

A green grand design hidden in the woods

Stanmer Park, Brighton BN1 9PZ
Tel: 01273 766631
www.lowcarbon.co.uk/earthship-brighton
Open for monthly tours and pre-booked courses and events
Bus 78

Hidden up a country lane a little way past Stanmer Park Nurseries is an unusual structure that resembles a Hobbit house. Called Earthship Brighton, this award-winning green building, surrounded by Soil Association accredited landscape, is one of two Earthships in the UK (the other is in Fife, Scotland) – and one of a few hundred around the world.

Earthships are buildings that set out to be genuinely sustainable and resilient in their local environment: designed to meet their own needs for water and energy, they are built from local, recycled and salvaged materials. If it's raining, they catch water; if it's windy, they generate free power; and if it's sunny, they capture free heat and electricity. Water conservation and energy efficiency are at the heart of the Earthship philosophy.

They're all based on the pioneering work of an offbeat architect called Mike Reynolds (who devised Earthship Biotecture) and the residents of three Earthship communities in Taos, New Mexico.

The Brighton project began in 2000 when Reynolds gave a public talk on Earthships in the city. This inspired a group of local people to plan an Earthship somewhere in the area – with a focus on green and progressive thinking and action.

To make their Earthship vision a reality, the group formed a non-profit organisation called the Low Carbon Trust. They then set about looking for a suitable bit of land on which to site their project. They eventually found a space belonging to a community group called Stanmer Organics, which also needed a meeting facility. Set on 7 hectares of council land in nearby Stanmer Park, Stanmer Organics was an ideal rural site for an Earthship.

Construction began in April 2003, when Reynolds and his crew from New Mexico visited for a week to build the "hut module" – the round room at the end of the building. During their visit, they trained local people in Earthship building techniques, including tyre ramming, glass-bottle brick making and clay plastering. The rest of the tyre walls were built over the summer, and the shell of the Earthship was completed by winter.

Today, it's open for tours and pre-booked courses. It can also be hired for events, including weddings.

24

URBAN FORAGING

Edible Brighton

At various locations in and around Brighton and Hove
www.schoolofthewild.com

We've all eaten plenty of picnics in Brighton parks and the surrounding countryside, but how about foraging for food, and even medicine, in these same places?

Brighton is an "edible city" – if you need convincing, take the fascinating half-day tour with the School of the Wild, which leads foraging walks in secret outdoor places around Brighton parks and up into the fringes of the South Downs.

Foraging trips are led by the school's team of expert foragers and herbalists and take place every few months. They typically start with an overview of foraging before the hunt for edible plants begins. During the walks, you're taught about the medicinal properties of the wild plants that grow freely around us, while you hunt and gather your own collection.

"Most people who come to our Bevendean foraging session have never heard of the garden we take them to," says Nigel Berman, founder of the School of the Wild. He started the business as a way to reconnect with the outside world and "help fix the broken relationship between people and the planet".

"It's remarkably easy to get here by bus from anywhere in Brighton, but hidden away at the end of a little path between two houses, you would never know the garden was there if you walk past it," he adds. "We also run foraging walks in Stanmer Park – another relatively unknown area hidden away from the main part of the park, which makes it exciting."

Within 2 metres of any tour route, a surprising number of edible and herbal plants can usually be found. "St John's Wort can easily be bought from a chemist, but most people don't realise that it's growing in abundance right here in the hedgerows," says Nigel. "And dandelions – these are everywhere but are considered invasive weeds, yet you can use every part to make all kinds of delicious herbal potions. Then there are wild garlic plants and hawthorn bushes full of little berries you can actually eat and that are really good for you."

After the hunting-and-gathering sessions, participants learn how to use what they find, turning the ingredients into drinks and preparations, to name but a few, and incorporate them into everyday life.

As well as foraging courses, the school runs events aimed at promoting a more mindful and natural existence, such as how to skin a rabbit, wild swimming, wood carving, and how to light a fire. It also occasionally runs foraging and wine-tasting courses in collaboration with the Brighton Wine Company.

25

WOODINGDEAN WELL

Deeper than the Empire State Building is tall …

Nuffield Hospital grounds, Warren Road, Woodingdean BN2 6DX

An international feat of engineering, Woodingdean Well occupies a bizarre yet ordinary setting in the Nuffield Hospital grounds, surrounded by a modern brick safety enclosure and covered with white mesh.

Arguably one of the most unusual local sites in Brighton, the little-known well is said to be some 390 metres deep and just 1.2 metres wide. Although several reports suggest it's the deepest hand-dug well in Great Britain – and perhaps even in the world – these claims are hard to verify. However, what is known is that it's deeper than the Empire State Building is tall – the famous New York landmark stands 1,250 ft (381 metres) high, to its roof.

In terms of its construction, historical records are sketchy and hard to come by, but contemporary sources claim that the well was built in 1858 to provide water for the local workhouse and Warren Farm Industrial School, and that it took men from the workhouse four years of perilous hard work to dig out by hand.

"The well is brick lined for the full height … platforms were constructed at various levels and recesses formed to accommodate the men working the winches to lower bricks and to raise the excavated material," explain local historians, Peter Mercer and Douglas Holland, in their book, *The Hunns Mere Pit*. "The shafts were lit by oil lamps and candles and, at the lower levels where air was insufficient, an air pipe provided enough air for the men's needs."

Eventually at around 392 metres, one of the builders reportedly felt the earth move beneath him, which suggested they'd struck water. Not surprisingly, it is said that they quickly scaled the shaft before the water rose around them, leaving no time to collect the equipment, which is apparently still in the well.

The hospital stands on the site of the old Warren Farm Industrial School, created to separate children from adults in the workhouse. It was built in December 1859, but it didn't open until there was a water supply – which would come from the well. The first inmates – 75 boys and 65 girls – marched from Dyke Road workhouse for their first day at Warren Farm on 14 August 1862. The school closed down when the workhouse system was abolished in 1930. The buildings have since housed a children's home, infant and junior schools, and a library. After a few years lying derelict, the buildings were demolished to make way for the Sussex Nuffield private hospital.

GLOBALLS JURASSIC MINIATURE GOLF

26

Glow-in-the-dark miniature crazy golf

Unit 8, Ground Floor, Mermaid Walk, The Waterfront,
Brighton Marina, Brighton BN2 5WA
Tel: 01273 911510
www.globalls.co.uk
Open: Mon–Thurs midday–10pm, Fri noon–11pm,
Sat 10am–11pm, Sun 10am–10pm

Crazy golf, mini golf, pitch and putt – whatever you want to call it, this miniature sport has been a popular seaside activity since the early 19th century. There are plenty of courses to choose from in Brighton, but none so unconventional as this new kid in town, which offers players an unusual take on the traditional game.

Launched in May 2016, Globalls at Brighton Marina is a miniature golf course with a difference – a 12-hole indoor ultraviolet mini golf course where players compete under the cover of darkness. Not only that, they get to time-travel back to the Jurassic period to putt their way past a series of life-size glow-in-the-dark dinosaurs.

Globalls was founded by Patrick and Julie Cosgrove, who came

up with the idea around Christmas 2015. "We were bored working as accountants," says Patrick, "so one day we just quit our jobs and said, 'Let's set up a glow-in-the-dark crazy golf course.' It really was as mad and as quick as that!"

Patrick grew up in Hastings, another British seaside town known for its crazy golf courses, but he felt the town lacked one with unique challenges and atmosphere. "This inspired me to go the extra mile," he says. As for the Jurassic Park theme? "That's simple. I just love dinosaurs," he adds.

He was keen that Globalls should be fun and unstuffy. "I wanted our course to look deceptively easy, so we've incorporated plenty of skill holes," he says. "The floor is uneven in places, which you can't see in the dark, and there are lots of tricks on the course to keep fooling you until you've played it a few times."

The couple worked closely with Brighton artist Sandy Moon to design the Jurassic-themed artwork. "She was a real gem to find. She helped us design the course that would tell a story as you make your way around, from T-rex stalking Triceratops to the volcanic eruption happening while dinosaurs fight as the asteroids hit our planet," says Patrick.

"Most people don't notice these quirks as they can't keep their eyes off the fluorescent UV dinosaurs. We also like to transform the course now and again to give people a different experience, like at Halloween and Christmas."

BRIGHTON WALK OF FAME

27

Brighton's answer to the Hollywood Walk of Fame

Palm Drive, The Waterfront, Brighton Marina, Brighton BN2 5WA
www.walkoffame.co.uk
Admission free

I t might occupy a less glamorous location than its transatlantic sister, the Walk of Fame on LA's Sunset Boulevard, but there's no doubt Brighton's version adds interest to an otherwise drab road in Brighton Marina.

It's easy to find on the south side of Palm Drive: look down and you'll see a line of square plaques set into the pavement that stretches for an entire block.

The Brighton Walk of Fame is the first-ever official walk outside of Hollywood – and the first of its kind in Britain. It consists of a trail of over 100 specially carved plaques bearing the names of stars and personalities with close connections to Brighton and Hove.

It was organised by Brighton-born musician David Courtney, who first had the idea in 1979 when he was living and working in LA as songwriting partner to Leo Sayer. It didn't become a reality until some 30 years later, which gave Courtney plenty of time to research Brighton's celebrity community and cultural history. He didn't restrict this to entertainers, but instead bridged the creative and cultural spectrum to include personalities from all disciplines. He then invited the public to vote for their favourites, rather than let a wealthy entertainment industry elite decide who should appear, as happens in Hollywood.

The plaques you see today are the result of that campaign. The Brighton Walk of Fame has continued to develop and grow since it opened in 2014, with new inductees added each year.

Brighton Music Walk of Fame

Courtney also plans to open a walk of fame on the Brighton Palace Pier to honour the many musicians, artists, composers and DJs closely associated with the city and Sussex from the early 1960s to present day. It will include 52 inductees in its inaugural year – The Who, Norman Cook, Jeff Beck, Rod Stewart, David Gilmour, Rizzle Kicks, Tom Odell and The Kooks to name a few – with further names added annually, all to be chosen by public ballot. For more information, visit www.walkoffame.co.uk/brighton-music-walk-of-fame.

28

DADDY LONG LEGS REMAINS

Remnants of Brighton's train in the sea

Undercliff Walk, Brighton Marina, Brighton BN2 5WA

Immediately east of Brighton Marina, at low tide, you might be lucky enough to spot a trail of concrete piles that marks the remains of Brighton's eccentric engineer, Magnus Volk's, most outlandish invention.

When Volk realised he couldn't extend his successful Volk's Electric Railway (see p. 40) further than Paston Place to Rottingdean, for various reasons, he turned his attention to a new venture: a completely new railway that would travel through the sea, called the Brighton and Rottingdean Seashore Railway.

Work on the project began in 1894 and involved building a railway across the rock pools between Brighton and Rottingdean. It was 5.5 metres wide to carry *Pioneer*, as it was originally called. This 45-tonne "salt-water tram" was supported on 7-metre-high struts, allowing it to travel through the water. With its gangly appearance, *Pioneer* quickly earned the nickname, "Daddy Long Legs".

Construction took two years and the railway officially opened on 28 November 1896. It was immediately popular but was destroyed in a storm only a week later. However, Volk started rebuilding it at once, including *Pioneer*, which had been knocked on its side. The railway reopened in July 1897 and carried 44,282 passengers in that year alone.

Daddy Long Legs faced constant difficulties, however. For example, the car slowed considerably at high tide, but Volk could never afford to improve the motors, while groynes built near the railway damaged the tracks and forced it to close for repairs at the height of summer. Immediately after reopening, Volk was told he'd have to divert his line so that the council could build a beach protection barrier. Without funds to do so, and to cut a long story short, Volk closed the railway. The track, car and other structures were sold for scrap, but some of the concrete sleepers can still be viewed at low tide.

Eventually Volk's Electric Railway was extended onshore, covering part of the same distance. It remains in operation today.

THE HEAD OF DAVID JACOBS

A reminder of Kipling Gardens' first gardener

Kipling Gardens, The Green, Rottingdean, East Sussex BN2 7HE
www.rottingdeanpreservationsociety.org.uk/the-kipling-gardens/
Open: April–Sept 9am–7pm, Oct–March 9am–4pm
Admission free

Set into a flint wall surrounding Rottingdean's magical Kipling Gardens is the sculpture of a head that even the village's long-time residents probably haven't noticed. You'll find this smiling stone face about 2 metres up on the left of the south entrance to the Rose Garden, and it makes for a surprising sight when you spot it.

In the 1980s, the Rottingdean Preservation Society saved the gardens from demolition after years of neglect, raising £51K to buy them. They then renovated them and handed them over to Brighton & Hove City Council, which opened them to the public in 1986.

The late David Jacobs was the first gardener employed by the council to work at the newly opened gardens. His legacy lives on in this stone relief sculpture by local artist, Janet Leech, who still lives in the village.

"David did a lot to create the garden we see today," says Valerie Whittle, vice-chairman of the Rottingdean Preservation Society. "He's said to have been responsible for many of the displays and for organising the donation of plants from people in the area to fill the beds."

Today, the gardens are a haven of tranquillity for everyone to enjoy, and a wander around reveals other curious treasures. These include a series of arched "windows" on the west wall – an old-fashioned garden feature known as a *claire-voie* – through which you can peer down onto the adjacent green below.

There's also a beautiful old renovated dovecote traditionally used to house pigeons or doves in the lower gardens.

Elsewhere, there's a fragrant Herb Garden, a Wild Garden complete with beehives, and a hidden corner called Roger's Nook full of ornamental grasses under-planted with blue and white alliums, which create a dramatic early summer display.

One of the most famous examples of a *claire-voie* is a round opening in a hedge of the White Garden at Sissinghurst Castle.

WISHING STONE

A mysterious symbol of local folklore

The Elms, The Green, Rottingdean, Brighton BN1

Some people think it looks like a gargoyle, others describe it as an imp, a hare, or even a grotesque human face. Whatever your take on it, this curious stone hidden amid the bricks on the outside wall of Rudyard Kipling's former home, The Elms, is one of the more obscure sights in picturesque Rottingdean – maybe even in Brighton.

The fact that it's set into a wall skirting the main road through Rottingdean, and that there's no pavement, makes it tricky to spot and awkward to reach. Once you've found it, the story goes that to make a wish – it mustn't involve money – you touch the stone's nose with your right forefinger, close your eyes and turn around three times away from the sun.

"It's not common knowledge today, although I've heard that some locals are still familiar with this belief," says local historian, Colin Manton. "Whether it works, I can't say for sure but I've heard some 'wishers' say that it does."

No one knows how the stone got here though it may have been unearthed from a pile of rubble in the churchyard of St Margaret's Church opposite. "The stone head might have been pulled out of the rubble of one or other church restoration, but I'm afraid it's all pure surmise," says Colin, "and I fear the stone's origin could prove elusive. I don't know whether it goes back any further or how it originated. That's the trouble with trying to research folklore – in the nature of things, folk didn't write it down!"

NEARBY
St Margaret's Church ㉛
The Green, Brighton BN2 7HA
Tel: 01273 301632
www.stmargaret.org.uk

Rottingdean's most historic other building is St Margaret's Church, thought to date from the early 11th century. It's built of flint and you'll find an almost exact replica at the Forest Lawn Memorial Park in Glendale, California. One of its most notable features is a set of seven stained-glass windows made by William Morris from designs by artist, Sir Edward Burne-Jones. Burne-Jones gifted the three windows on the east, to commemorate the marriage of his daughter Margaret, here in the church: they depict three archangels, Gabriel, Michael and Raphael.

THE KIPLING ROOM

An ode to Rottingdean's celebrity resident

The Grange, The Green, Rottingdean, Brighton BN2 7HA
Tel: 01273 301004
www.rottingdeanpreservationsociety.org.uk/the-grange/
Open: Mon–Fri 10am–4pm (closed Wed), Sun 1pm–4pm

With its chocolate-box cottages built around the green, and a pretty pond, the picture-postcard village of Rottingdean is a more genteel alternative to hedonistic Brighton.

One of its most beautiful houses is called The Elms. Built in 1750, it was once the home of Rudyard Kipling, who rented the house for 3 guineas a week from 1897 to 1902. It was here that he lived with his wife and family and that he wrote *Stalky & Co*, Kim and some of his famous *Just So* stories.

On the other side of the green, in a whitewashed Georgian mansion called The Grange, you'll find a room dedicated to the writer's life and work, which includes a quirky recreation of his study.

Although the bizarre waxwork of Kipling sitting at his desk might come as a shock, the Victorian-style banker's desk filled with all kinds of curios is a joy to browse: there's an original Royal Standard 10 typewriter, traditional ink fountain ink pots and pens in their holders, a blotter pad, brass desk lamps, smoking pipes on little wooden trays, stocks of old candle wax, handwritten letters on The Elms headed notepaper, a wooden ruler and old faded newspapers.

There are also shelves filled with novels and personal ornaments, and a stand complete with a globe, walking stick and Kipling's traditional safari hat. Two walls of black and white family photos of the author's time at The Elms show his children riding bikes and playing in the garden. There's a map of Kipling's world, a family tree and a cabinet devoted to HMS Kipling.

Brighton on the big screen

Also at The Grange, don't miss the "Cinema by the Sea" room dedicated to Brighton as a film setting. It celebrates local actress Dora Bryan, and includes an article from *The Times* magazine with Audrey's Hepburn's first photoshoot – taken in Rottingdean in 1951.

The Kipling Gardens

After Kipling left The Elms, it was rented out until Sir Roderick Jones, chairman and managing director of the world-famous Reuters News Agency, bought it in 1929. After he died, the gardens became derelict, but were saved and turned into Kipling Gardens (see p. 280), now open to the public.

BALSDEAN ABANDONED VILLAGE

Remembering a forgotten community

Just outside Woodingdean, east of Brighton
Buses 52 from Brighton station and 22A from Churchill Square stop nearby

Hidden in a secluded valley on the fringes of the city in the South Downs National Park is an abandoned village – although you can't actually see it.

Balsdean is just one of some three thousand deserted settlements scattered around Britain and evacuated by the military during the Second World War. It's said to date back to medieval times.

In the 18th century, it was a thriving agricultural hamlet based around two farms, Sutton and Norton. It included a few outbuildings, two cottages and a chapel dating back to the 12th century, later used as a barn.

The village was depopulated towards the end of the medieval period and the chapel had fallen out of use by the 16th century. Norton Farm, however, thrived up until the early 19th century before being turned into a lunatic asylum.

It was then evacuated just before the First World War, leaving Sutton Farm, which by this point had become Balsdean Farm. It survived until 1939, when the occupants were asked to leave so that the valley could be turned into a camp for the Canadian Army. All the buildings were subsequently used for target practice and reduced to rubble by 1945.

As a result, there is now little evidence of Balsdean's existence except the remnants of a pump used to take water from a well on Norton Farm and a plaque commemorating the site of the Norman chapel which reads, "This marks the site of the altar of the Norman church of Balsdean".

The abandoned barns we see today are the remains of a farm built after the Second World War to replace Balsdean Farm.

A musical ghost walk

In 2012, Brighton band Grasscut released the album 1 Inch: ½ Mile designed to accompany a walk around the ghost village of Balsdean. It starts at the edge of the suburban housing estate of Woodingdean and descends through the rolling downland into Balsdean, taking in the scattered remains of the village. You can listen to the album and download a map of the walk from the band's website at www.grasscutmusic.com/1inch.

This area of the South Downs National Park is also home to several remarkable archaeological sites. They include a burial mound on Bullock Hill, a Bronze Age cemetery and a protected earthwork enclosure at the Bostle, and an area of rare uncultivated downland at Castle Hill, which has been designated a National Nature Reserve.

HARVEY'S CROSS

Brighton's smallest cemetery

Pickers Hill, Pickers Farm, Saltdean, South Downs National Park

Perched on its own atop a hill beside a bridleway on Pickers Hill near Saltdean is a lone monument – albeit overgrown and in disrepair.

It's what's become known as Harvey's Cross: a memorial to a man named Colonel John Harvey from Bedfordshire, said to have died in a riding accident here in 1819 aged just 48 – ironically, this was allegedly during a stay in Sussex to improve his health and wellbeing.

Historical documents claim he graduated from Cambridge University and was a family man with five children: a son and four daughters.

There are conflicting contemporary accounts as to how Harvey met his death. According to local historian, Douglas d'Enno, "On 21 June 1819, the *Sussex Weekly Advertiser* recorded that he 'fell from his horse in a fit' while other sources mention a weak heart, a heart attack and death in the heat of the chase."

The memorial was erected by his family in 1873 and depicts a white marble cross mounted on a two-stepped base. An inscription reads: "John Harvey ESQ. of Ickwell Bury in the county of Bedford died suddenly on this spot on the 20th day of June 1819".

The cross gradually fell victim to the ravages of time and was used for military target practice in the Second World War – it's thought to have been destroyed by Canadian soldiers billeted in Rottingdean and Saltdean. By the mid-1990s, it was cracked, chipped, split, full of holes and in need of some attention.

Concerned for the monument's upkeep, d'Enno and John Harvey's descendants raised £4,000 to restore it, adding a protective fence, a commemorative bench and another plaque which reads: "This plaque commemorates the restoration of Harvey's Cross on 20 June 1999 by the Harvey family to perpetuate John Harvey's memory and preserve the heritage of downland".

The restored monument was unveiled in 1999 by the Lord Lieutenant of East Sussex, Admiral Sir Lindsay Bryson, although the memorial we see today has been destroyed once again after vandals apparently smashed it with a hammer.

This discovery is the perfect addition to a walk around the abandoned village of Balsdean (see p. 286).

Unusual Bars, Cafés and Restaurants

1. COLONNADE BAR
2. ENGLISH'S OF BRIGHTON
3. MARWOOD BAR AND COFFEEHOUSE
4. OLD SHIP HOTEL DINING ROOMS (PICTURED ▲)
5. PAVILION GARDENS CAFÉ
6. ROYAL PAVILION TEAROOM
7. THE CURIOUS MR HANBURY
8. THE QUADRANT
9. 1909
10. CAFÉ & SALVAGE
11. DECCAN TIFFIN
12. THE BEE'S MOUTH
13. THE REGENCY TOWN HOUSE DINING CLUB
14. UNITHAI
15. WORLD PEACE CAFÉ
16. BOM-BANE'S

17 PROUD CABARET
18 THE BLACK DOVE
19 BRIGHTON NOW CAFÉ
20 HELL'S KITCHEN
21 ROCK*OLA COFFEE BAR
22 THE GALLERY
23 THE GREEN DOOR STORE
24 THE REAL JUNK FOOD PROJECT
25 BALCONY BAR
26 BARDSLEY'S OF BAKER STREET
27 LOVING HUT
28 BRIGHTON YOGA SUPPER CLUB
29 MEDITERRANEO
30 SMORL'S HOUMOUS FALAFEL & SALAD BAR
31 THE COWLEY CLUB

CENTRAL BRIGHTON

① COLONNADE BAR

10 New Road, Brighton BN1 1UF
Tel: 01273 328728 • www.thecolonnadebrighton.co.uk
Quirky bar next door to the Theatre Royal (see p. 72), with a good selection of gins and an eccentric decor, including a bar upholstered in crushed velvet and walls full of framed photos of theatre actors and actresses.

② ENGLISH'S OF BRIGHTON

29–31 East Street, Brighton BN1 1HL
Tel: 01273 327980 • www.englishs.co.uk
Brighton's oldest restaurant, spread across three former fisherman's cottages and well known for its fish and seafood dishes.

③ MARWOOD BAR AND COFFEEHOUSE

52 Ship Street, Brighton BN1 1AF
Tel: 01273 382063 • www.themarwood.com
Café known for its eccentric decor featuring old film props and lots of crazy bric-a-brac. Open for coffee and cakes during the day and cocktails in the evening.

④ OLD SHIP HOTEL DINING ROOMS (PICTURED ◀)

The Old Ship Hotel, King's Road, Brighton BN1 1NR
Tel: 01273 329001 • www.thecairncollection.co.uk/hotels/the-old-ship/
This quirky dining room and bar lie deep beneath Brighton's oldest hotel, dating back to the 16th century (see p. 70), in a vast complex of old smugglers' tunnels. The rooms are mainly open for private dining events but occasionally open to the public for cocktail parties.

⑤ PAVILION GARDENS CAFÉ

29 New Road, Brighton BN1 1UG
Tel: 01273 730712 • www.paviliongardenscafe.co.uk
Founded in the 1930s by Mr Herbert Tennet, this family-run café started life as a wooden refreshment hut by the Palace Pier but moved to the Pavilion Gardens in the 40s. It was rebuilt in the Art Deco-style kiosk we see today in the 1950s and is still going strong.

⑥ ROYAL PAVILION TEAROOM

4/5 Pavilion Buildings, Brighton, BN1 1EE
Tel: 03000 290900 • http://brightonmuseums.org.uk/royalpavilion/visiting/
eat-and-drink-at-the-royal-pavilion/
Entry to the Royal Pavilion also unlocks access to this opulent second-floor tearoom, serving traditional British afternoon tea, sandwiches and cakes. Its balcony overlooks the Pavilion Gardens.

⑦ THE CURIOUS MR HANBURY

Artist Residence Hotel, 33 Regency Square, Brighton BN1 2GG
Tel: 01273 324302 • www.mrhanburybar.co.uk

A secret cocktail bar hidden behind a bookshelf in the basement of the Artist Residence Hotel. There's no menu to choose from – instead, cocktails are made bespoke according to your preference that night.

⑧ THE QUADRANT

13 North Street, Brighton BN1 3GJ
Tel: 01273 733238 • www.quadrant.pub

Relaxed and atmospheric historic bar open since 1864. It's also home to The Clock Tower Cinema, which shows cult movies every Monday for free, including free popcorn (see p. 62).

⑨ 1909

26–27 East Street, Brighton BN1 1HL
Tel: 01273 778674 • www.1909brighton.co.uk

Pressleys has transformed the space above its ground-floor jewellery shop into a sophisticated restaurant few people know is there. Serving small seasonal plates and organic wines for lunch and dinner.

HOVE

⑩ CAFÉ & SALVAGE

84 Western Road, Hove BN3 1JB
Tel: 01273 323884

Brighton is packed with quirky independent coffee shops, but this one stands out from the crowd for its interior filled with random thrifted finds and salvage.

⑪ DECCAN TIFFIN

32 Westbourne Villas, Hove BN3 4GF
Tel: 01273 749619 or 01273 103779 • www.decantiffin.co.uk

Supper clubs featuring nostalgic cuisine from the royal kitchens of the princely states and Mughal rulers, and from ordinary homes and the streets of India, hosted by Priya in her grand Hove villa.

⑫ THE BEE'S MOUTH (PICTURED ▶)

10 Western Road, Hove BN3 1AE
Tel: 01273 770083

If there were an award for the Brighton pub with the quirkiest decor, it would surely go to The Bee's Mouth for its unusual features. These include a pulpit in the downstairs nook, a extensive collection of Steve Buscemi pictures and a basement cinema room.

⑬ THE REGENCY TOWN HOUSE DINING CLUB

The Regency Town House, 13 Brunswick Square, Hove BN3 1EH
Tel: 01273 206306 • www.rth.org.uk

Dine like it's the Regency period at this regular quirky supper club, which takes place in The Regency Town House dining room or sometimes in the basement kitchen. It's hosted by food historian and Regency Town House volunteer, Paul Couchman, and is based on authentic historical dishes. The ticket price includes two courses, Regency punch, claret and port. All profits go towards the ongoing restoration of the building.

⑭ UNITHAI (PICTURED ◀)

10 Church Road, Hove BN3 2FL
Tel: 01273 733246

This is a Thai supermarket but walk through and, hidden at the back of the shop, you'll find a Thai café that looks like a cosy dining room. The food is delicious, authentic and served fast.

⑮ WORLD PEACE CAFÉ

Bodhisattva Centre, 3 Lansdowne Road, Hove BN3 1DN
Tel: 01273 732917 • http://meditateinbrighton.com/world-peace-cafe-shop/

A vegan Buddhist café in the heart of Hove. See p. 118 for the Bodhisattva Kadampa Meditation Centre.

KEMPTOWN

⑯ BOM-BANE'S

24 George Street, Brighton BN2 1RH
Tel: 01273 606400 • www.bom-banes.com

Eccentric café-restaurant and performance venue named after its owner, Jane Bom-Bane. It serves homemade food for lunch and dinner and hosts film nights, live music and puppetry shows. Jane also performs after dinner every Friday and Saturday night on request.

⑰ PROUD CABARET

83 St George's Road, Brighton BN2 1EF
• www.proudcabaretbrighton.com

Dinner and live entertainment in a former mausoleum (see p. 154).

⑱ THE BLACK DOVE

74 St James's Street, Brighton BN2 1PA
Tel: 01273 671119 • www.blackdovebrighton.com

An independent, laid-back pub with a fascinating decor. It's known for its acclaimed cocktails, features an intriguing underground drinking den and hosts DJ nights.

NORTH LAINE

⑲ BRIGHT NOW CAFÉ

Brighthelm Centre, North Road, Brighton BN1 1YD
Tel: 01273 821512 • www.brighthelm.org.uk/cafe

Airy community café inside the striking John Wells-Thorpe-designed brutalist building (see p. 178). Enjoy homemade food while you browse the gallery of local art that fills its walls.

⑳ HELL'S KITCHEN

4 Gardner Street, Brighton BN1 1UP
Tel: 01273 604925 • www.hellskitchendeli.co.uk

A Brighton institution passed down through three generations. Established in 1951 as a New York-style deli, it serves the same dishes as it did originally – including its famous latkes, and salt beef, spinach and feta rolls.

㉑ ROCK*OLA COFFEE BAR (PICTURED ▶)

29 Tidy Street, Brighton BN1 4EL
Tel: 01273 673744 • www.rockolacoffeebar.com

Pastel-coloured diner café, filled with 1950s memorabilia and serving all the classic diner dishes, like hotdogs and onion rings in baskets. Named after its fabulous Rock*Ola jukebox crammed with records of the time, which are free to play.

㉒ THE GALLERY

Brighton Metropolitan College, Whitecross Street, Brighton BN1 4FA
Tel: 01273 667711 • www.gbmc.ac.uk/brighton/college-life/
campuses-and-facilities/the-gallery

Hospitality and catering students deliver fine-dining-quality food and service to members of the public for lunch and dinner during the week in this little-known training restaurant.

㉓ THE GREEN DOOR STORE

Lower Goods Yard, Brighton train station, Brighton BN1 4FQ
• www.thegreendoorstore.co.uk

Live music venue set under Brighton station in a railway yard with a late bar every night and free entry. Look for the green door.

㉔ THE REAL JUNK FOOD PROJECT

• www.therealjunkfoodproject.org

"Pay As You-Feel", pop-up lunchtime cafés hosted in various quirky venues around Brighton and Hove, such as One Church in Gloucester Place (check the website). All dishes are made out of surplus food from supermarkets and restaurants that would otherwise go to waste.

LONDON ROAD

㉕ BALCONY BAR
Duke of York's Picturehouse, Preston Circus, Brighton BN1 4NA
Tel: 0871 902 5728 • www.picturehouses.com/cinema/Duke_Of_Yorks
The country's oldest operating cinema (see p.170) is also home to a cool balcony bar, where you can enjoy pizza, wine and craft beer, with a close-up view of its famous can-can legs.

㉖ BARDSLEY'S OF BAKER STREET
22–23a Baker Street, Brighton BN1 4JN
Tel: 01273 681256
Open since 1926, this is arguably the best chippy in Brighton and Hove. Boasts a dining room filled with Max Miller memorabilia (see p. 190).

㉗ LOVING HUT
The Level, 5 St Peter's Place, Brighton BN1 4SA
Tel: 01273 689817 • thelevel.lovinghut.co.uk
Delicious, wholesome vegan food served in a small café set in what was once one of Brighton's First Divisional police stations.

㉘ BRIGHTON YOGA SUPPER CLUB (PICTURED ▼)
The Studio, Whippingham Road, Brighton BN2 3PF
• www.downwarddogyoga.co.uk • www.rhubarbandbeans.com
Not many people know about this yoga studio in an old restored church hall just off Elm Grove. For one Sunday every month, it becomes the setting for a secret girls-only yoga supper club, featuring 90 minutes of relaxing yoga led by Helen Moss followed by a three-course vegan feast catered for by vegan chef, Lorraine Counsel, of Rhubarb & Beans.

㉙ MEDITERRANEO

2A Clyde Road, Brighton BN1 4NP
Tel: 01273 674350 • www.mediterraneorestaurants.co.uk
The perfect neighbourhood gem of a restaurant that you want to keep a secret. Inside is like stepping into what you might imagine a little traditional Sicilian village restaurant to be – small, cosy, crammed with tables bathed in candlelight. The food is delicious, authentic and homemade.

㉚ SMORL'S HOUMOUS FALAFEL & SALAD BAR

Open Market, Marshall's Row, Brighton BN1 6JU
Tel: 01273 626315
It all started with a brand of delicious Brighton-made houmous. Now the team behind Smorl's has expanded into their own food outlet in the eccentric Open Market. They serve up delicious Ottolenghi-inspired falafel boxes for lunch, complete with generous helpings of their houmous.

㉛ THE COWLEY CLUB

12 London Road, Brighton BN1 4JA
Tel: 01273 696104 • www.cowleyclub.org.uk
A cooperative socialist centre named after local activist, Harry Cowley. It's a community vegan café and bookshop by day and a members' bar by night.

ALPHABETICAL INDEX

33 PALMEIRA MANSIONS	116
AIDS MEMORIAL SCULPTURE	134
ANGEL OF PEACE STATUE	14
ANNA'S MUSEUM	52
ANTIQUE SAFE AT THE DUKE'S	170
ART DECO BUS SHELTER	94
ATHINA-B ANCHOR	34
ATTREE VILLA TEMPLE	142
BACKSTAGE AT THE BOOTH MUSEUM	248
BALSDEAN ABANDONED VILLAGE	286
BENJAMIN JAMES SMITH HOUSE	196
BLACKROCK SUBWAY STUDIOS	44
BODHISATTVA KADAMPA MEDITATION CENTRE	118
BONE GUILLOTINE	232
BOOTH MUSEUM OF NATURAL HISTORY	246
BRIGHTON AND HOVE PÉTANQUE CLUB	15
BRIGHTON DOME BACKSTAGE TOURS	78
BRIGHTON GREENWAY1	68
BRIGHTON HIPPODROME	66
BRIGHTON MUSIC TUNNEL	28
BRIGHTON PALACE PIER HERITAGE TRAIL	30
BRIGHTON TOY AND MODEL MUSEUM	174
BRIGHTON WALK OF FAME	276
BRIGHTON'S VICTORIAN SEWERS	26
CAMDEN TERRACE	172
CERES SCULPTURE	76
CHATTRI MEMORIAL	224
CONSTABLE'S FORMER HOME	50
DADDY LONG LEGS REMAINS	278
DINO THE ELEPHANT SCULPTURE	210
DOROTHY STRINGER SCHOOL BUTTERFLY HAVEN	228
DR RUSSELL PLAQUE	98
EARTHSHIP BRIGHTON	268
ELECTRIC LIGHTING PLAQUE	18
EUGENIUS BIRCH PLAQUE	20
EVEREST'S GRAVE	110
FABRICA GALLERY	64
FEIBUSCH NATIVITY MURAL	138
FISHERMEN'S GALLERY	150
FLINT GROTTO	36
FLORENCE PLACE JEWISH BURIAL GROUND	262
FOREDOWN TOWER	202
FORMER HOME OF MARIA FITZHERBERT	96
FORMER ISETTA FACTORY SITE	184
FRENCH PROTESTANT CHURCH	56
GLOBALLS JURASSIC MINIATURE GOLF	274
HARVEY'S CROSS	288
HEADLESS STATUE	124
HENRY SOLOMON PLAQUE	80
HOLLINGBURY HILLFORT	264
HOVE LAGOON MODEL YACHT CLUB	212
HOVE PARK MINIATURE RAILWAY	218
INDIA GATE	86
IRELAND'S GARDENS GATEWAY	192
JAIPUR GATE	108
JEW STREET	180
K6 PHONE BOXES	254
KEMP TOWN RAILWAY TUNNEL	148
LITTLE FRIDGE LIBRARY	132
LOAVES AND FISHES SCULPTURE	178
MADEIRA DRIVE GREEN WALL	42
MADEIRA LIFT	38
MAGNUS VOLK'S FORMER OFFICE AND WORKSHOP	40
MAX MILLER ROOM	190
MAX MILLER STATUE	74
MIDDLE STREET SYNAGOGUE	68
MILE OAK FARM	200
"MURMURATION" AERIAL SHOW	24
BOOTH MUSEUM OF NATURAL HISTORY	248
OLD POLICE CELLS MUSEUM	82
OLD SHIP ASSEMBLY ROOMS	70
ORNATE INTERIOR OF THE SACRED HEART CHURCH	112

PATCHAM PEACE GARDEN	226	THE CLARENCE SUITE	22
PEEL FAMILY CRYPT	152	THE DRAWING CIRCUS	88
PORTSLADE MANOR RUINS	204	THE GARDEN HOUSE	188
PRESTON MANOR PET CEMETERY	240	THE GHOST OF JENNY LIND SCULPTURE	164
PRESTON MANOR WALLED GARDEN	242	THE GOLDSTONE	220
PRESTON MANOR	230	THE HEAD OF DAVID JACOBS	280
PRESTON WELL HOUSE	238	THE HOVE CLUB	114
PRINNY'S PIANO	92	THE JUGGLER STATUE	115
QUADROPHENIA ALLEY	84	THE KIPLING ROOM	284
RACEHILL COMMUNITY ORCHARD	158	THE OLD VICARAGE	182
REGENCY DRAGONFLIES	260	THE PEPPERPOT	140
RICHARD'S GARAGE	256	THE REGENCY TOWN HOUSE	122
RICHARDSON'S YARD	166	THE SKY LOUNGE	16
ROUND HILL CATS' CREEP	193	THEATRE ROYAL BACKSTAGE TOURS	72
ROYAL CREST	234	TIME BALL	62
ROYAL PAVILION BASEMENT AND TUNNELS	90	TOMB TRAIL	136
ROYAL SPA REMAINS	146	"TWINS" SOUND-AND-LIGHT SCULPTURE	58
ROYAL SUSPENSION CHAIN PIER REMAINS	32	UNIVERSITY OF BRIGHTON DESIGN ARCHIVES	102
SASSOON MAUSOLEUM	154	URBAN FORAGING	270
SCHOOL OF SCIENCE AND ART TERRACOTTA FRIEZES	100	WASTE HOUSE	104
SECRET GARDEN KEMP TOWN	160	WATERLOO STREET ARCH AND GARDEN	126
SECRET GARDEN	208	WEST BLATCHINGTON WINDMILL	216
SHOE TREE	194	WESTERN PAVILION	48
SILVER ALTAR	186	WHITEHAWK HILL	156
ST ANDREW'S CHURCH	128	WILD PARK	266
ST LUKE'S VICTORIAN SWIMMING BATHS	144	WINSTON CHURCHILL PLAQUE	120
ST MARGARET'S CHURCH	283	WISHING STONE	282
ST MARYE'S CONVENT BURIAL GROUND	206	WOODINGDEAN WELL	272
ST NICHOLAS REST GARDEN BURIAL VAULTS	54	WRITE AROUND AIR STREET ART STORY TRAIL	60
ST PETER'S CHURCH	236		
STEVE OVETT'S FOOT	252		
SUSSEX MASONIC CENTRE	176		
TAKE SHELTER! MUSEUM	258		
THE "PRESTON TWINS"	244		
THE CASCADE	250		
THE CIRCUS PROJECT	214		

PHOTOGRAPHY CREDITS

Emma Croman: Art Deco Bus Shelter, Benjamin James Smith House, Brighton Hippodrome, Jew Street, Max Miller Statue, Middle Street Synagogue, Old Ship Assembly Rooms, Royal Pavilion Basement and Tunnels, Prinny's Piano, 33 Palmeira Mansions, Rock Ola Café, Sacred Heart Church, Sussex Masonic Centre, The Hove Club, Theatre Royal.

Lyndsey Haskell: Antique Safe in the Lobby of the Duke's, Attree Villa Temple, Backstage at the Booth Museum of Natural History, Bodhisattva Kadampa Meditation Centre, Bone Guillotine, Brighton Greenway, Brighton Pier Heritage Trail, Brighton Toy and Model Museum, Camden Terrace, Dino the Elephant, Embassy Court, Everest's Grave, Fishermen's Gallery, Florence Place Jewish Burial Ground, Foredown Tower, French Protestant Church, Headless Statue, Hollingbury Hillfort, Hove Lagoon Model Yacht Club, Hove Park Miniature Railway, Jaipur Gate, Kemp Town Railway Tunnel, Little Fridge Library, Madeira Drive Green Wall, Madeira Lift, Max Miller Room, Mile Oak Farm, Old Police Cells Museum, Patcham Peace Garden, Peel Family Crypt, Portslade Manor Ruins, Racehill Community Orchard, Richardson's Yard, Remains of The Royal Spa, Royal Crest, Silver Altar at St Bartholomew's Church, St Andrew's Church, Steve Ovett's Foot, St Luke's Swimming Baths, St Nicholas Rest Garden and Burial Vaults, The Booth Museum of Natural History, The Garden House, The Goldstone, The Headless Statue, The Kipling Room, The Pepper Pot, The Secret Garden Kemp Town, St Marye's Convent Burial Ground, Tomb Trail, Write Around Air Street, Waterloo Street Arch and Garden, Whitehawk Hill, West Blatchington Windmill, Wild Park.

Lucy Sharpe: AIDS Memorial Sculpture, Angel of Peace Statue, Anna's Museum, Athina B Anchor, Brighton Music Tunnel, Brighton Walk of Fame, Dr Russell Plaque, Flint Grotto, Former Isetta Factory Site, Henry Solomon Plaque, India Gate, Ireland's Gardens Gateway, Jenny Lind Ghost Train Sculpture, K6 Phone Boxes, Lampposts of St George's Church, Loaves and Fishes Sculpture, Madeira Lift, Maria Fitzherbert's House, Music Mural, Preston Manor Pet Cemetery, Preston Manor Walled Garden, Quadrophenia Alley, Richard's Garage, Sassoon Mausoleum, Shoe Tree, St Peter's Church, Steve Ovett Statue, The Cascade, The Old Vicarage, The Preston Twins, Time Ball, Twins Sound and Light Sculpture, Western Pavilion.

Dan Seymour: Balsdean Abandoned Village, BlackRock Subway Studio, Chattri Memorial, Churchill Plaque, Daddy Long Legs Remains, Eugenius Birch Plaque, Harvey's Cross, Preston Well House, The Head of David Jacobs, Richardson's Yard Green Roofs, The Secret Garden Hove, The Wishing Stone, The Woodingdean Well.

Attree Villa Temple © James Gray Collection
Brighton Dome © Jim Stephenson
Brighton Locomotive Works © James Gray Collection
Ceres sculpture © Antony McIntosh
Daddy Long Legs © Royal Pavilion & Museums, Brighton & Hove
Earthship Brighton © Mischa Hewitt
Electric Lighting Plaque © JJ Waller
Feibusch Mural © Sandra South
Henry Solomon © Royal Pavilion & Museums, Brighton & Hove
Ireland's Gardens © Royal Pavilion & Museums, Brighton & Hove
Isetta © Wikipedia
Jew Street © James Gray Collection
John Constable Self Portrait © Wikicommons
Kemp Town Railway Station © James Gray Collection
Magnus Volk's Former Office and Workshop © Lucy Williams
Murmuration © Andrew Forsyth
Regency Dragonflies © Kate Benjamin
Richard's Garage © My Brighton & Hove
Royal Suspension Chain Pier © Royal Pavilion & Museums, Brighton & Hove
Royal Suspension Chain Pier Remains © Dominic Alves on Flickr, Creative Commons
Sir Albert Sassoon © Wikicommons
School of Science and Art Terracotta Friezes © Barbara Taylor
The Clarence Suite © Hilton Brighton Metropole
The Drawing Circus © Mary Martin
The Goldstone © James Gray Collection
The Royal Spa © The Regency Society
University of Brighton Design Archives © Barbara Taylor
Urban Foraging © Nigel Berman / School of the Wild

ACKNOWLEDGEMENTS

Phil Armstrong, Paul Couchman, Dan Danahar, Nick Dwyer, James Farrell, Austen Gayton, Suzanne Hinton, Lee Ismail, Craig Johnson, Al Mackintosh, Jackie Marsh-Hobbs, Judy Middleton, Kevin Newman, Jo Nightingale, Abigail Rawlings, David Seidel, Eddie Seymour, Sue Shepherd, Jake Spicer, Barbara Taylor, Jemma Treweek, Nick Tyson, Kevin Wilshire, Paula Wrightson, and my friends and family for their enthusiasm and support.

Maps: Louisa Keyworth, Layout design: Coralie Cintrat, Layout: Nicola Erdpresser, Proofreading: Jana Gough and Eleni Salemi